Immaterial Labor and Cultural Production

Immaterial Labor and Cultural Production:

The Dialectic of Late Capitalism

By

Sílvio Camargo

**Cambridge
Scholars**
Publishing

Immaterial Labor and Cultural Production:
The Dialectic of Late Capitalism

By Sílvio Camargo

This book first published 2023

Cambridge Scholars Publishing

Lady Stephenson Library, Newcastle upon Tyne, NE6 2PA, UK

British Library Cataloguing in Publication Data
A catalogue record for this book is available from the British Library

ISBN (10): 1-5275-9397-5
ISBN (13): 978-1-5275-9397-8

For
Maria Ferraz da Silva Camargo
(In memoriam)

...but that out of the construction of a configuration of reality the demand
for its
[reality's] real change always follows promptly.
—Theodor W. Adorno

CONTENTS

PREFACE TO THE ENGLISH EDITION

This work was originally written as a doctoral thesis just over ten years ago and published as a book for the first time in Brazil. In my country, at that time, the concept of immaterial labor was still little known and naturally encountered a lot of resistance, especially in the field of thinkers that Moishe Postone called traditional Marxism. While I was writing the work at times it seemed to me that what I was talking about something more visible in countries like the United States or Europe than in my own country, although today I no longer see this distinction as clearly as the new characteristics of world capitalism. Instead of being an aged text, I see it as more current than ever.

For approximately two decades I dedicated myself to the study of themes and theoretical problems related to Critical Theory, or for those who prefer, the so-called Frankfurt School, and in my first book, also published in Portuguese, I analyzed the impact of Theodor W. Adorno in contemporary social theory, emphasizing the relationship between modernity and domination. The problem of domination continues to be the epicenter of this book *Immaterial Labor and Cultural Production: the dialectic of late capitalism*, but in a certain sense the conceptual and theoretical reflection is also a diagnosis of the time.

What is in question is the very history of capitalism and its configuration at the present time. Ten years after the original writing of this book, some things have changed, both in historical reality and in the ideas of some authors analyzed. Among those who are alive, Axel Honneth was the one who most changed his way of doing theory in the last ten years. As far as the historical reality is concerned, empirical examples that I provide, especially about technologies, may already seem outdated for the new generations, but this was also already foreseen, and this book also deals with this process of accelerated technological transformations.

Regarding the original version in Portuguese, I tried to keep the text with minimum changes in relation to the Brazilian edition, making the citations and references based on the languages in which the works were originally read, translating to English when this is not the language original. André Gorz's works especially had been read in Brazilian editions. And speaking of countries and languages, from the Global North and South, it is important to emphasize that contrary to the prevailing view in the academic field, especially that of the Social Sciences, here in the South we also try to do *social theory*. As the Frankfurtians thought, doing social theory is also resisting the incessant process of capitalist domination.

Porto Alegre, July 2022.

INTRODUCTION

The work presented here aims to elucidate and, at the same time, problematize the category of immaterial labor, understanding that this category is historically constituting itself as something central to the processes of capitalist wealth production and capital accumulation, which have characterized world capitalism over approximately the last three decades. The emergence of immaterial labor as something central in the current capitalist historical formation is shown as a new issue of investigation for social theory, and our purpose is to present the thesis that capitalism in its current stage has been constituting forms of domination and sociability characterized by the junction, by the intertwining, between culture and immaterial labor, which is the current dialectic of late capitalism.

Contemporary social theory, in recent years, has witnessed an already extensive debate as to whether we are living in a new stage of world capitalism that began in the mid-1970s. The designations for the changes that take place in capitalism in this historical period, however, are varied and controversial. There are authors who do not even advocate the concept of capitalism as fundamental to the understanding of this historical period, as is the case of those who use expressions such as post-industrial society[1], consumer society[2], network society[3] among other designations. On the other hand, there are those who support the concept of capitalism, be it late [4], cultural[5] or cognitive[6].

At the center of such debate and such changes is the category of labor and its statute for understanding contemporary society. The idea of the end

---

[1] Daniel Bell, *The Coming of Post-Industrial Society* (New York: Basic Books, 1999).

[2] Jean Baudrillard, *The Mirror of Production* (St. Louis: Telos Press, 1975).

[3] Manuel Castells, *A Sociedade em Rede* (A era da informação. Vol. I. São Paulo: Paz e Terra, 2006).

[4] Fredric Jameson, *Pós-Modernismo. A Lógica Cultural do Capitalismo Tardio* (São Paulo: Ática, 1997).

[5] Jeremy Rifkin, *A Era do Acesso* (São Paulo: Makron Books, 2001).

[6] Yan Moulier-Boutang, *Le Capitalisme Cognitif* (Paris : Éditions Amsterdam, 2007).

of the labor society or the exhaustion of the production paradigm[7] will find a certain similarity in recent attempts to theorize the notion of immaterial labor, since this concept would be the new basis of production of wealth, so that understanding it has become an essential theoretical task for those who also seek to understand the current transformations of world capitalism. But this similarity, as we intend to suggest, is only shown in some precise aspects regarding the understanding of the labor category, since the field of investigation about the immaterial will end up showing quite different theoretical positions regarding the transformations taking place in contemporary society.

The debate on immaterial labor has as its main theoretical references André Gorz, Antonio Negri and Maurizio Lazzarato. André Gorz has a long and controversial contribution to the Sociology of Work, with his most recent work *O Imaterial* [8] being one of the starting points for our investigation. Negri and Lazzarato[9] belong to another tradition of thought that began with Italian workerism and currently incorporates a strong influence from French post-structuralism. We prefer to group these two authors, somewhat arbitrarily, for the purposes of clarity of exposition, under the slogan of thinkers of *Multitudes*, to which are added thinkers such as Yann Moulier-Boutang, Carlo Vercellone, Antonella Corsani, and several others.[10]

On the other hand, the problems proposed here can also be addressed by thinkers who do not even use the concept of capitalism, or late capitalism, such as Daniel Bell and Manuel Castells, who have other points of reference for understanding this historical stage of Western civilization, not necessarily using the concept of immaterial labor, and not even capitalism. However, among other significant contributions, they also strive to elucidate the role of knowledge and information for an understanding of the world of labor and contemporary culture. We shall, therefore, also consider such contributions, showing the theoretical affinities and differences between them and the authors of *Multitudes*.

---

[7] Jürgen Habermas, O *Discurso Filosófico da Modernidade* (Lisboa: Dom Quixote, 1998).

[8] André Gorz, *O Imaterial* (São Paulo: Annablume, 2005).

[9] Maurizio Lazzarato e Antonio Negri, *Trabalho Imaterial* (Rio de Janeiro: DP & A editora, 2001).

[10]This option is due to the fact that these thinkers regularly publish in the French magazine *Multitudes*, in our opinion the main source of consultation and intellectual production around the concept of immaterial labor. A considerable part of its main collaborators was also part of the magazine *Futur Antérieur*.

The changes that are taking place in capitalism, by some also called world globalized, or financial capitalism, point, according to our point of view, to the need to recover the concept of late capitalism, proposing that it is possible to update this concept from the problematization of the immaterial labor category. Late capitalism, which since the 1940s had different meanings, today takes on a quite different form, in the face of which new reflexive parameters are required regarding the problems of domination and emancipation, the historically inspiring theoretical problem of critical theory of society. This theory, in its Frankfurtian version, had already detected since the 1930s that the Marxian conception of domination, centered on class domination, needed a modification, considering the contributions of Nietzsche, Weber and Lukács, to a concept of instrumental rationality.[11] Consequently, at that moment, the classical Marxian perspective of emancipation based on labor itself was also exhausted, at least from the point of view of Critical Theory.

Not only Critical Theory, but a growing number of theorists of society began to diagnose the processes of domination in contemporary society in a sphere that is no longer that of labor and the theory of value itself. Such a diagnosis includes a wide range of theories of the new social movements, which point to spheres such as culture, or the lifeworld, as the basis for new emancipatory possibilities for humanity. Here, distinct positions stand out, such as those of Jürgen Habermas and André Gorz. This shift in perspective, which some designate as post-socialist, is also the basis for recent attempts in Critical Theory to propose other categories that elucidate the conflicts and experience of individuals in an advanced capitalism, this being the position, for example, of Axel Honneth and his theory of recognition.

These theoretical changes and controversies, which have taken place in contemporary social theory, have as their substrate the understanding that significant changes have taken place in capitalism, especially since 1973, marking a new stage in its history. Based on our thesis that this stage has been characterized by a tendency to prominence, and even a centrality of immaterial labor, we present as a general hypothesis the idea that we are experiencing a transition phase in the capitalist mode of production. The direction that such transformations will take in the future is still uncertain, and it is up to us to outline some aspects of the present, of the transformations of contemporary society, which point out the possible consequences of this historical trend.

---

[11] About this concept, see: Sílvio Camargo, *Modernidade e Dominação: Theodor Adorno e a Teoria Social Contemporânea* (São Paulo: Annablume/Fapesp, 2006).

As for this present, our understanding is that the so-called immaterial labor is only understandable as something inseparable from the cultural sphere, resulting in the impossibility, under present conditions, of an effective separation between labor and culture.[12] This idea contradicts several of the so-called two-dimensional theories of society and approaches the dialectical tradition, passing through Theodor Adorno and Fredric Jameson, whose theoretical positions are that the concept of totality remains the best critical category for the analyses of capitalism in terms of its own concept. Notwithstanding the readings of contemporary culture in terms of postmodern culture, one of our arguments will be that it is possible to understand the intertwining between culture and immaterial labor in a concept of post-culture industry.

In this way we intend to investigate the existing relations between immaterial labor and cultural production based on three fundamental axes: a) material labor itself increasingly depends on the counterpoint of immateriality even within the scope of industrial production. It refers to the fact that the capacities of communication, information, cooperation, and use of the intellect become central to the production process. The demand for a greater intellectual qualification of workers indicates the need for them to use knowledge and *savoir*[13] that are related to a cultural context in which such knowledge is developed and which is acquired and processed not only in the physical and temporal space of the labor activity; b) the process of capitalist accumulation, and even the production of goods, has acquired a growing tendency towards an expansion and homogenization of the service sector, but also towards a centrality of consumption, marketing, advertising, knowledge and of the information that come to determine the new economic relations. Such activities, considered immaterial, directly involve human subjectivity, insofar as it is through the establishment of cultural patterns of consumption and individual and collective behaviors that the production of wealth takes place. Economic production, before being materialized, and

---

[12]Although the idea of entanglement between market and culture has already been postulated at different times in contemporary social theory, our perspective takes as a reference the concept of labor, and not of the market, pointing to an interpretation, in our understanding, differentiated in terms of placement of the theoretical problem to be developed.

[13] From chapter 2 of this book, it will be better explained why we chose to keep the original word *savoir* from the French language, especially as used by André Gorz, who has in Portuguese (the original language of the author of this book) the equivalent of *saber*. This sense differs from "knowledge" of the English language, and this difference concerns crucial theoretical issues for the arguments developed here in this book.

even when it is not, depends directly on what is produced as a culture. This means that immaterial labor is not only related to a new stage of capitalism, but the hypothesis suggested here is that it also refers to a new stage in the processes of social domination. Contemporary culture and immaterial labor come to represent the new *locus* of capitalist legitimation and domination; c) contradictorily, the tendency towards the immateriality of labor also points to the possibility of a reduction in labor time and the configuration of a "mass intellectuality." From theorists such as Habermas and Gorz, we know that it is through a non-instrumental rationality, situated in the lifeworld (*Lebenswelt*), that it would be possible to constitute a new utopia and emancipatory project for humanity. This implies that the reduction of labor time acts directly on the possibility of an expansion of actions that are processed in the lifeworld and in the sphere of culture, those that for them can break with the processes of domination, that is, the immaterial also brings the gestation of new utopian possibilities. On the other hand, Gorz presents, like other theorists, the possibility of making use of the concept of experience as something significant for the problematization of the utopian.

The results of our investigation will be present in four argumentative steps, which are organized into eight small chapters, or excursions, in the following order: in the first chapter we present some of Marx's ideas, extracted mainly from the *Grundrisse*,[14] to show the plausibility of adopting him as a theoretical starting point for the problematization of the immaterial labor category. We will try to show how in this work the relationship between time and value as conceived by Marx makes it possible to talk, more than a century later, about immaterial labor. We start from the presupposition, therefore, that a critical theory of capitalism has Marx as one of its essential points of reference. In the second chapter, we will continue this argument, but now showing how the category of the immaterial emerges in contemporary social theory, mainly from the works of Gorz and Negri, and how we can conceptualize the possibility of immaterial labor still based on Marxian thought.

Having placed the thesis of the immaterial, in chapters 3 and 4 we try to show that its historical effectiveness requires us to reflect on the understanding of the very concept of capitalism, or the capitalist mode of production, in this historical phase that we are considering. In the third chapter, we discuss how it is possible to think about this historical stage by recovering the concept of late capitalism, of Frankfurtian origin, to re-elaborate it in the face of the conditions present at the beginning of the 21st

---

[14] Karl Marx, *Grundrisse: Foundations of the Critique of Political Economy* (Middlesex: Penguin Books, 1989).

century. Although the existing definitions prove to be insufficient, the critical model of understanding capitalism presented by Adorno and Jameson, remains extremely present today. In the fourth chapter, we expose the hypothesis of cognitive capitalism, which comes from a French tradition of thought, and which relates this concept of capitalism to the idea of the immaterial. In order to do so, we problematize the notion of knowledge considering other contributions of contemporary theory.

In the fifth chapter we seek to problematize the notion of subjectivity, which has become theoretically crucial both for understanding the meaning of immaterial labor and for understanding the cultural transformations of contemporary society. A theme that goes back to the very origins of modern philosophy, the relationship between the concepts of subjectivity and intersubjectivity become a central part of the investigation essential for the understanding of late capitalism. In the sixth chapter of the work, we develop our central hypothesis: that immaterial labor and contemporary culture must be thought of together, in the face of that new subjectivity that has been developing in the capitalist world in the last three decades. Instead of privileging the notion of postmodernity as Jameson does, we understand that parallel to the initial argument of the first chapter, about the *Grundrisse,* regarding the historical tendency towards a post large-scale industry, today we experience a kind of "post-culture industry", which retains numerous aspects of the thought of Adorno and Horkheimer,[15] but at the same time shows the exhaustion of the idea of culture thought from the concept of industry.

In the last two chapters we problematize the original idea of a Critical Theory that is the relationship between domination and emancipation. In chapter 7 we will try to show how modern forms of domination continue to exist in a late capitalism informed by the immaterial, but at the same time, how it is also necessary to extend the ideas of exploitation and injustice to the present. In this sense, we understand that late capitalism in a transitional phase has brought to light new forms of exploitation, mainly in the form of self-exploitation, which do not replace the broader concept of domination but are integrated into it.

In our last chapter, we only indirectly thematized the problem of emancipation, leaving it latent, by suggesting that the concept of experience is now fundamental for a critical theory of society. In this sense, we start principally from André Gorz and Axel Honneth, to try to show that there is in this concept, at the same time as a critique of the present, a utopian

---

[15] Theodor Adorno e Max Horkheimer, *Dialética do Esclarecimento* (Rio de Janeiro: Zahar, 1985).

element that should not be overlooked, but that helps theory inform of an immanent critique to protect the subject's position.

CHAPTER 1

IMMATERIAL LABOR AND THE *GRUNDRISSE*

Marx's conception of history, which has its first developments from the writings that deal with the critique of Hegel's *Philosophy of Right*,[16] is concerned with showing that human labor, initially as an ontological category and later as an anthropological and analytical one, characterizes the evolutionary process of human sociability based on the transformation of nature by man and also on the constitution of relationships and interaction among human beings.[17] Between the *Economic-Philosophical Manuscripts* (1844),[18] through *The German Ideology* (1847)[19] to the *Grundrisse* (1857), a conception of history matures that increasingly shifts its attention from a terminology typical of the Hegelian Left to consolidate itself as a critique of political economy, or that is, as the dialectical critique of the capitalist mode of production, and the status of human labor in the specific circumstances of this mode of production. And it is evident that *Capital* represents the complete maturation of his thought.

One of the significant issues that appears, however, in the *Grundrisse* and does not emerge with the same clarity in other texts by Marx, not even in *Capital*, is the historical fate of the labor category itself in a no longer capitalist historical formation.[20] Inquiring about the place that human labor

---

[16] Karl Marx, *Crítica da Filosofia do Direito de Hegel* (Lisboa: Estampa, 1983).

[17] On this second aspect, Habermas disagree. See for exemple: Jürgen Habermas, *Para a Reconstrução do Materialismo Histórico* (São Paulo: Brasiliense, 1990). Habermas, like other authors, understands that the dimension of social interaction is not present in the Marxian conception of history, in which labor would only manifest the dimension of instrumental actions.

[18] Karl Marx, *Manuscritos Econômico-Filosóficos* (Lisboa: Ed.70, 1980).

[19] Karl Marx and Frederick Engels, *The German Ideology* (New York: International Publishers, 1977).

[20] We privilege here, especially in this first chapter, passages from Marx's *Grundrisse*, as we understand that in this work there are elements to think about both immaterial labor and questions related to value and laboring time. In this case, it follows the appropriations already made by Postone, Marcuse, Gorz and others. We do not share the position that only *Capital* expresses the maturity of Marxian thought.

would have in a post large-scale industry or even socialist transition society does not mean merely a speculation situated in the field of philosophy of history but brings at its center the very debate around the characterization of the capitalist mode of production. Furthermore, when thinking about the normative dimension of the theory, it is necessary to be clear, when undertaking the critique of capitalism, about what place human labor occupies in the configuration of human sociability.

Contemporary discussions about immaterial labor have brought in the treatment given to it by its main theorists, certain awfully specific references regarding Marxian thought and its driving position of the very concept of immaterial. The debate about the immaterial arises, for those who have been willing to theorize it in recent years, as a problem clearly situated on the horizon of the Marxist tradition.[21] This concerns not only the fact that it is capitalism itself that is being problematized as a concept, but also the fact that it is through the Marxian categories of value, abstract labor, productive forces and relations of production that we can also problematize the concepts of immaterial and capitalist mode of production.

The understanding that labor in the context of the critique of political economy is criticized by Marx with reference to a specific historical context immediately establishes the premise that capitalist relations of production, as he understands them, do not fundamentally relate to an ontological apprehension of labor. Although this form of apprehension is also present in Marx's thought, we understand that the category of labor, as presented in the *Grundrisse*, aims to elucidate the capitalist mode of production, which as such shows certain historical specificities as to the way in which men produce their lives, and start determined social relationships:

> In the succession of economic categories, as in any other historical, social science, it must it not be forgotten that their subject – here, modern bourgeois society – is always what is given, in the head as well as in reality, and that these categories therefore express the forms of being, the

---

See also: Anthony Giddens, *A Contemporary Critique of Historical Materialism*, vol I. (Berkeley: University of California Press, 1987).

[21]We refer here mainly to André Gorz and Antonio Negri, whose theorization of the immaterial constitutes a permanent dialogue with the Marxian work, even if it is to criticize it. But as we highlighted in the "Introduction" above, central aspects of the theories developed by them find some correspondences in authors such as Bell, Lévy or Rifkin, who in no way come close to the Marxist tradition. As we propose to understand the *transformations of capitalism* from the meaning of immaterial labor in contemporary society, one of the developments of this theoretical effort will also be a reflection on the relevance of Critical Theory in the face of such transformations.

characteristics of existence, and often only individual sides of this specific society, this subject, and that therefore this society by no means begins only at the point where one can speak of it *as such; this holds for science as well.*[22]

As other theorists considered classics of social theory, industrial society appears as the historical and reflexive basis of all Marxian critique, but such a historical substrate from the materialist point of view cannot have any other concept than that of capitalism. However, it is evident that the emergence of large-scale industry is the empirical correlate of such a concept and the contribution to the construction of the theory of value, the categories of alienation and commodity fetishism, the class struggle and the processes of circulation and accumulation of capital. The use of the concept of capitalism as equivalent to the historical process of industrialization passed through the sieve of a critique of capitalism that had manufacturing as its first historical moment. But it is the relationships characteristic of large industry that will serve as a basis for the development of the main Marxian categories.

But from the outset, we must note that for Marx, industrialism does not have the same meaning as capitalism. For Marx, the capitalist mode of production, and the specific characteristics pertinent to it, can only be overcome when that set of attributes specific to the industrial mode of production is also overcome. For Marx, changes in the mode of distribution are distinct from changes in production.[23] In this way, we can question the thesis according to which the end of capitalism is only equivalent to the end of private ownership of the means of production and the establishment of a planned economy, no longer subject to the irrational mechanisms of the market. The form of property and state or collective economic planning are necessary but insufficient conditions for overcoming capitalist domination and its mechanisms, even economic ones, typically capitalist.[24]

It is necessary to be clear that production is not equivalent to distribution. And the overcoming of capitalism, to constitute free relations, must mean the end of the industrial mode of production itself as representative of a certain stage of development of the productive forces.

---

[22] Marx, *Grundrisse*, 106.

[23] Ibid., 832.

[24]Some authors, including Charles Bettelheim and Harry Braverman, have shown how in the former USSR all industrial standards were reproduced since the beginning of the revolution and the Taylorist model of labor organization (with Lenin's consent) remained unchanged the patterns of capital accumulation in typically capitalist molds. See: Harry Braverman, *Trabalho e Capital Monopolista* (Rio de Janeiro: Zahar, 1981).

The end of private property, and the private appropriation of wealth, will continue to sustain the characteristics of capitalist domination, case in a society, even if socialist, industrial and wage labor persist. The alteration of the mode of distribution does not *per se* equate to the end of the mode of production, which should be the aim of socialists. As says Moishe Postone in his analysis of the *Grundrisse*:

> This section of the *Grundrisse* makes abundantly clear that the overcoming of capitalism for Marx involves the overcoming of the capitalist mode of production based on value – the expenditure of direct human labor time – as the social form of wealth. Moreover, and this is crucial, what would be involved is a total transformation of the material form of production, of the way people work. *The overcoming of "the mode of production founded on wage labor" appears to involve the overcoming of the concrete labor by the proletariat.*[25]

The *form of property* appears to Marx as something that concerns distribution, which leads us to understand that the end of private property does not necessarily mean changing the mode of production, as the productive forces cannot simply be identified with the own production mode:

> Labour cannot become play, as Fourier would like, although it remains his great contribution to have expressed the suspension not of distribution, but of the mode of production itself, in a higher form, as the ultimate object.[26]

The problem posed by the *Grundrisse*, which calls our attention, is precisely about the possibility of capitalism's survival in a social formation that we could call "post large-scale industry." And it is from this interpretation that some of the controversies regarding immaterial labor arise. Although our reading of the set of Marxian thought indicates that the dimension of a historical and revolutionary subject is always present in it, the peculiarity of this work by Marx is precisely in pointing out the indications as to the probable end of industrial production as a result of the very advance of the productive forces. This advance would reach such a point where the meaning of labor as the effective producer of wealth would be radically altered.

The *Grundrisse* present a lot of Marxian insights not taken up with the same emphasis in the writing of *Capital*, for example, questions we

---

[25] Moishe Postone, "Necessity, labor and time: a reinterpretation of the Marxian critique of capitalism." *Social Research,* no 45 (Winter 1978): 748-9.
[26] Marx, *Grundrisse*, 712.

understand to be central to understanding capitalism more than a century after Marx's death. One of them, as stated above, is the need to distinguish between wealth and value. But this labor also has aspects of what we could call a utopian dimension, precisely when Marx proposes to talk about the possibility of a future that would mean the complete historical negation of the present moment, that is, of a wealth founded on labor time.[27] We understand that the apparent extrapolations that Marx makes in this work, if we compare them with the whole of his thought,[28] only demonstrate the tensions and even contradictions that are expressed in a thought that has always called itself a form of "critique" and therefore, averse to dogmatism.

We understand that the mode of production category is the key to understanding capitalism in Marxian terms, and precisely the point of disagreement between a considerable part of contemporary theorists who point to the exhaustion of the production paradigm. The unveiling and critique of the capitalist mode of production will, however, also encompass a normative dimension, which Gramsci referred to as the philosophy of *praxis*, and on the other hand a philosophy of history inspired by Hegel.[29] The dialectical category of totality, emphasized by Lukács of *História e Consciência de Classe*,[30] places in the scope of wage labor, with emphasis on factory work, the dimension of human life in which the processes of alienation and domination are constituted, but also the normative horizon of an emancipation of humanity that is primarily the emancipation of the

---

[27]Although it is not our purpose to discuss the meaning of the concept of utopia in Marx, we understand the following passage as very suggestive: "If between 1845 and 1848 there was a great separation between bourgeois society and utopias, it is important to define the difference between Critical Communism and Utopia from the outset that the theory of Marx and Engels was situated on the same side of the barrier as Utopia, outside bourgeois positivity, on the side of absolute distance, and that it was only on this side that it could confrontation arises. If the critique of Marx and Engels revealed the 'weaknesses' of utopia, it took its strengths for granted," Miguel Abensour, *O Novo Espírito Utópico* (Campinas: Ed. Unicamp, 1990), 31.

[28] Benhabib very accurately highlights that, among the passages we are analyzing here from the *Grundrisse,* if compared with excerpts from the famous text on commodity fetishism in vol. I of *Capital* leads us to two distinct ways of perceiving this utopian (transcendent) moment of Marxian critique. See: Seyla Benhabib, *Critique, Norm, and Utopia* (New York: Columbia of University Press, 1986), 128.

[29] The normative and historical dimension of Marx's thought indicates one of the crucial points of differentiation between his thought and what Max Horkheimer called Traditional Theory. For the different shades of contemporary logical positivism, such as pragmatism and the Vienna circle, these aspects of Marx's thought place him in the wake of the metaphysical tradition of modernity.

[30] Georg Lukács, *História e Consciência de Classe* (Lisboa: Escorpião, 1986).

producing class, the proletariat, bearer of a revolutionary *praxis* that is restored to the instance of truth about the course of the historical process.

Such a proletariat would have the destiny of asserting itself as a collective subject, capable of revolutionizing the means of production by abolishing wage labor and the social division of labor, eliminating capitalist domination. The emancipatory dimension of Marxian thought appears in this way as linked to human labor. Emancipation means radically modifying the division and labor relations, assuming that in a liberated society, labor relations endowed with meaning and human self-fulfillment would be established.

It so happens that in the *Grundrisse,* with emphasis on the chapter entitled *Contradiction between the foundation of bourgeois production (value as measure) and its development,* Marx[31] develops his conception of industrial society from which we can learn that the modification of relations of production can only lead to the moment of human self-realization to the extent that such relations cease, at the same time, to be based on industrial relations of production, since the development of the productive forces immanent in industrial development lead to their own overcoming, and, as is happening, we will no longer have human labor, in capitalist molds, as the central category in the production of society's wealth. This interpretation of the Marxian text thus opposes the ontological argument defended by broad sectors of Marxism, which see human emancipation necessarily as an emancipation of the proletariat in the sphere of labor itself.

This means that labor in an emancipated society would represent the very end of labor in the way it was created in industrial society, that is, as the main producer of value, associated, in industrialism, with a certain stage of development of the productive forces. To think, therefore, that human emancipation means emancipation through labor, leads us to an incongruity if we think that the tendency of capitalist development is that this labor, understood in this way, will no longer be the main source of wealth in a society of post-large-scale industry. According to Marx:

> But to degree that large-scale industry develops, the creation of real wealth comes to dependent on labor time and on the amount of labor employed than on the power of the agencies set in motion during labor time, whose 'powerful effectiveness' is itself in turn out of all proportion to the direct labour time spent on their production, but depends rather on the general state of science and on the progress of technology, or the application of this science to production.[32]

---

[31] Marx, *Grundrisse*, 704.
[32] Ibid., 704-705.

This passage, as we will see later, serves as a reference for some of the main thinkers of immaterial labor. Its statement, for now, serves to situate our starting point: that in Marx's *Grundrisse* we find numerous reflections on a possible exhaustion of human labor, in the molds of industrialism as the grounding of wealth.

For many Marxists of 20th century, whom Perry Anderson called Western Marxists,[33] with special emphasis for the tradition of Critical Theory, the Marxian conception of an emancipation processed from the world of labor, and the role of the proletariat, began to lose its impact since the first decades of the century, as a result not only of possible limitations of the Marxian theoretical construction, but as a result of the own experiences and historical transformations that are evident in capitalist societies. The limitation, therefore, of that conception of an emancipatory labor does not refer exclusively to the already famous Habermasian diagnosis of the aging of the production paradigm,[34] but already in the first decades of the 20th century the first generation of Frankfurtians elucidated the historical and theoretical fragility of such a conception.

For Marx, in all his work, capitalist domination is fundamentally class domination, domination is thus always at the same time its manifestation as exploitation. The proletarian is the wage worker who produces capitalist wealth, in the form of value, and finds himself disjunct both from the result of his labor and from the way in which it is constituted. The alienated subject is an appendix of the machine. This class domination and the concomitant alienation of the proletariat are understandable within the framework of a theory of value. It is important, however, not to oversimplify this Marxian conception of class domination, as Marx refers to a mode of production, which in its own abstraction is intended to make domination possible:

> In Marx's analysis, social domination in capitalism does not, on its most fundamental level, consist in the domination of people by other people, but in the domination of people by abstract social structures that people themselves constitute. Marx sought to grasp this form of abstract, structural domination – which encompasses, and extends beyond, class domination – with his categories of the commodity and capital.[35]

What constitutes value, in turn, is the human labor time employed in the production of commodities. It is known, then, that it is the labor time that

---

[33] Perry Anderson, *Considerações Sobre o Marxismo Ocidental* (São Paulo: Brasiliense, 1989).

[34] Jürgen Habermas, *O Discurso Filosófico da Modernidade*, 81-8.

[35] Moishe Postone, *Time, Labor, and Social Domination* (London: Cambridge University Press, 2003), 30.

measures the value of commodities, constituting abstract labor, and that promotes the formation of surplus-value and capital accumulation. For Marx, in short, human labor time spent in the production of commodities is the founding nucleus of capitalist wealth itself, in the form of value, wealth that is founded on abstract labor:

> Furthermore, the different use values are the product of the activities of different individuals, therefore the result of works differentiated by their individual character. But as exchange values, they represent equal, undifferentiated work, that is, work in which the individuality of workers is erased. Labor that creates exchange value is, therefore, *abstract general labor*.[36]

Time, for Marx, thus appears not only as an abstraction that operates at the level of a philosophy of history and through which it is possible to speculate on the course of humanity, or, as in the case of Hegel, of the spirit. Time is a category of critique of political economy, something whose objectivity is manifested by human *praxis* that forms a materialistically interpreted history, objectivity that is expressed by human action, which is inseparable from the very concept of value. Time is a category of social theory and the comprehensive core of capitalist society. As we will see later, understanding the so-called immaterial labor is understanding the transformations of temporality in contemporary society.[37]

In the works of Marx produced from the mid-1850s onwards, the ground of his critique of political economy begins to form, wherein his appropriation and critique of Ricardo and Proudhon constitute the elements that will become central in *Capital*. Marx first tries to clarify the way in which the value of commodities is constituted, showing that such determination is constituted by labor, that is, it will be the time spent by workers for the production of a commodity, as abstract labor, which elucidates the apparent exchange of equivalents in capitalism:

> You will recollect that I used the word "*Social* labour," and many points are involved in this qualification of "Social." In saying that the value of a commodity is determined by the *quantity of labour necessary* applied or crystallized in it, we mean the amount of *labor necessary* for its production in a given state of society, under certain social average conditions of

---

[36] Karl Marx, *Contribuição para a Crítica da Economia Política* (Lisboa: Estampa, 1977), 37.

[37] These transformations in the dimension of contemporary temporality are associated with changes that also occur in the dimension of spatiality, as for example: Edward W. Soja, *Geografias Pós-Modernas* (Rio de Janeiro: Zahar, 1993).

production, within a given social average intensity, and average skill of the labour employed.[38]

The postulation of abstract labor as the basis of value will become problematic when we are confronted with those passages from the *Grundrisse* that inform us about the tendency to exhaust the industrial mode of production. In several passages of the *Grundrisse* Marx suggests that with the advance of the productive forces by the large-scale industry, a very evident tendency to decrease the human labor time used in the creation of value develops, in the capitalist mode of production. Since value, by definition, is what is constituted through labor time, we would have, within the scope of Marxian thought itself, on the one hand, a problem regarding the interpretation of his work, and, on the other, theoretical elements that could help us in understanding capitalism in its current stage. According to Marx:

> [...] The *theft of alien labor time, on which the present wealth is based,* appears a miserable foundation in face of this new one, created by large-scale industry itself. As soon as labour in the direct form has ceased to be the great well-spring of wealth, labour time ceases and must cease to be its measure, and hence exchange value [must cease to be the measure] of use value. *The surplus labour of the mass* has ceased to the condition for the development of general wealth, just as the *non-labour of the few*, for the development of the general powers of the human head.[39]

The concept of *general intellect* refers to a certain degree of development of capitalism in which abstract knowledge, both scientific in nature and not only of a scientific nature, comes to occupy the role of the main productive force in the form of a diffuse intellectuality that replaces those forms of repetitive labor performed by the proletariat.[40] We would be talking,

---

[38] Karl Marx, *Wage Labour and Capital/Wages, Price and Profit* (Paris: Foreign Languages Press, 2000), 78-9.

[39] Marx, *Grundrisse*, 705.

[40] In the view of Paolo Virno this knowledge is objectified in fixed capital and embodied in the machinery system itself, while for Vercellone when we transpose this diffuse intellectuality to the context of the crisis of Fordism, it also refers to processes of massification of education that also make its existence possible. See: Virno, Paolo, "The Ambivalence of Disenchantment." In *Radical Thought in Italy*, ed. Paolo Virno and Michael Hardt (Minneapolis: University of Minnesota Press, 1996), 13-36. See also: Carlo Vercellone, "É na reversão das relações de saber e poder que se encontra o principal fator da passagem do capitalismo industrial ao capitalismo cognitivo". Entrevista *Revista IHU online*, 216, abril 2007a. https://www.ihuonline.unisinos.br/artigo/21-artigo-2007/852-carlo-vercellone-1

therefore, about something no longer measurable even in terms of abstract labor:

> The development of fixed capital indicates to what degree general social knowledge has become a direct force of production, and to what degree, hence the conditions of the process of social life itself have come under the control of the general intellect and been transformed in accordance with it.[41]

We will come back to this concept later. For now, it should be noted that capital, in principle, can only expand and accumulate within the capitalist mode of production, since it is only in capitalism that, as a labor force, is effectively a commodity. Meanwhile, the value of commodities, whose determination is in the *quantum* of human labor embodied in them, is only valued, and becomes capital as a result of this human labor force employed in its production.

However, in a historical situation in which labor time would no longer be the main constituent of value, the question to be posed is how capital continues to be valued and how accumulation takes place. The peculiarity of the *Grundrisse* lies precisely in questioning the circumstance of the possible exhaustion of the model of large-scale industry, but the interpretation of the Marxian text, as always, is not simple. One of the controversial issues that will arise between upholders and detractors of the category of immaterial labor is that concerning the very end of capitalism. Is it possible, for example, to speak of a "communism of knowledge" within capitalist production relations?[42]

There are passages from the *Grundrisse,* but also from *Capital itself,* that point to the fact that value, founded on exchange value and abstract labor, is a specific historical form of production of wealth, which only takes place in the capitalist mode of production. In this way, the production of value is inseparable from wage labor. Without it, there would be no way for capital to appreciate. However, in *the Fragment of Machines* Marx suggests that value and wealth are different things, and that the emergence of post large-

---

[41] Marx, *Grundrisse*, 706.

[42] We will re-develop this notion of "knowledge communism" in the chapters ahead. For now, it is worth summarizing the issue: the authors who defend immaterial labor as the new main productive force no longer have in their normative arguments the *telos* of a revolutionary process that will lead to socialism. The transformation of society takes the form of reforms in capitalism, which may even point to its overcoming. The objection raised by some tendencies of Marxism is that capital only expands and accumulates through the appropriation of the labor of others, that is, as long as there is capitalism, there is validity of the labor theory of value. For it to cease to exist, a socialist society would be necessary.

scale industry would imply that science and technique would become the central elements of production, and no longer wage labor. It seems evident to us, in favor of traditional Marxists, that this assumption of Marx's is an insufficient element to speak of the existence of communism within capitalism, but as we will see later, the arguments mobilized by authors such as Negri and Gorz in favor of the so-called knowledge communism refer not only to the Marxian theoretical scope.

As the productive forces develop, the general tendency of capitalism is to produce wealth with an ever-smaller amount of living labor, that is, the use of variable capital.[43] The living labor time used in production tends to decrease, at least as far as the logic of production relations is concerned, in an inverse proportion to the growth of constant capital, notably of machinery. This is within a model of industrial production, because in the immaterial regime, in post-industrial production, fixed capital (machinery, equipment, real estate) cannot be considered in the same way as it was in the large-scale industry. In post-industrial production, the exact opposite occurs, the accumulation of wealth would not occur either through the direct appropriation of other people's labor time, nor through the sum of material goods instrumentalized in production,[44] but only through the capitalist's ability to have information and knowledge that places it in a privileged position within the production chain.

We understand that in a reading of the *Grundrisse*, having as reference the questions historically posed by Critical Theory,[45] we see that Marx's thought must be understood as a historical analysis of capitalism, and, therefore, the category of labor is understood, as it would have been for Marx, as a category to be criticized within the framework of the capitalist mode of production. That is, we start from capital and capitalism to understand labor and not the other way around. It can be said that labor is seen as an analytical and not an ontological category. According to Marx:

> Labor seems to be a very simple category. The idea of labor in this universality – as labor in general – is also one of the oldest. However,

---

[43] In Negri's view, the labor force was transformed from variable capital to fixed capital.

[44] The dematerialized form that characterizes current financial capital is one of these aspects. Another is the one pointed out by Jeremy Rifkin regarding the replacement of material possession by the mere use of what once constituted the fixed capital of large industry. Renting, for example, has become more important than owning, as the very use of wealth is changing. It has become more advantageous, for example, to rent a car than to acquire it, as well as machinery, equipment, real estate, etc. See: Rifkin, *A Era do Acesso*.

[45] Specially, Postone, *Time, Labor, and Social Domination*.

conceived from an economic point of view in this simple form, *labor* is as modern a category as the relations that this simple abstraction engenders.[46]

On the next page:

This example of the labor clearly shows that even the most abstract categories, although valid – precisely because of their abstract nature – for all epochs, are no less, in the determined form of this same abstraction, the product of historical conditions and they are only fully valid under these conditions and within their framework.[47]

Our understanding is that the mature Marx's enterprise is to criticize the capitalist mode of production, apprehending as its core a production of wealth that embodies the labor theory of value, that is, value emerges as the critical category that serves to demystify the social relations of domination within a given historical period. As we know, however, for Marx capitalism is not the end of history, on the contrary, the very advance of the productive forces that come into contradiction with the social relations of production foreshadows its crisis and the possibility of overcoming it.[48]

From this understanding, it follows that since capitalism is the mode of production that is identified with the production of value, whose social content is always a relationship of domination, the issue will become much more complex when the constitution of value through labor time begins to decrease in the framework of capitalism itself. And here we are not talking about the production of wealth in a society, of capitalist wealth, but about the value that is one of its specific manifestations:

The opposition between real wealth and labor time should be noted. To emphasize what may be an unnecessary point, value for Marx is a historical rather than a natural or suprahistorical category of social wealth. Marx has written a 'critique' of political economy, and value is to be understood as a critical category: one with which the foundations of the form of wealth

---

[46] Marx, *Contribuição para a Crítica da Economia Política*, 232.

[47] Ibid., 233.

[48] In the *Grundrisse* we capture the way in which Marx analyzes the problem of the social division of labor in the history of capitalism, introducing the distinction between formal and real subsumption, a distinction also clearly outlined in Chapter VI of *Capital*. In the view of one of the authors who make up the arguments in chapter 4, further on, the notion of *general intellect* is understood as a third term, subsequent to the moment of real subsumption, and capable of elucidating the present historical stage of capitalism, in which the *general intellect* would also represent a third historical moment in terms of social division or labor. See: Karl Marx, *O Capital,* Capítulo VI-Inédito (São Paulo: Moraes, 1985b), 87-120.

specific to capitalism are revealed and yet which – in its dynamic – reveal the *historicity* of that form. Beyond a certain historical stage, value becomes less and less adequate as a measure of wealth, that is, capitalist relations of production become increasingly anachronistic in terms of the productive forces to which they gave rise.[49]

While the material wealth of a society can be measured by the number of products produced and is shown as a function of several factors such as knowledge, social organization, and even natural conditions, in addition to value itself, the latter directly refers to labor time human that constitutes it. For Marx, as passages from *Fragment of Machines* clearly show, the material production of wealth, based on the creation of value, will have its limitation placed by the very advance of the productive forces, which does not necessarily mean, as Negri will say, that from them the formation of a new mode of production will immediately follows. The Marxian argument is that the advancement of science and technology implies a decrease in the time required for the production of commodities, that is, the human labor time spent in their production. Live labor, manual or intellectual, is gradually reduced to tasks of control and surveillance, reducing the need for labor in the production process. The logical consequence of this decrease is also the reduction in the number of hours of living labor to be used in production, which starts to have in the operation of machines, and in the application of science and technology, its main source of wealth production. The theory of value then finds its own limit, insofar as the appropriation of other people's labor time, wage labor itself, tends to cease to exist:

> In this transformation, it is neither the direct human labor he himself performs, nor the time during which he works, but rather the appropriation of his own general productive power, his understanding of nature and his mastery over it by virtue of his presence as a social body – it is, in a word, the development of the social individual which appears as the great foundation-stone of production and of wealth.[50]

This possibility of a historical limit to the law of value is at the heart of the critique made against the theorists of immaterial labor, which unfolds into three main objections: First, in the case of those who identify immaterial labor with services, the objection will be made that these, for Marx, do not constitute productive labor. Second, only wage labor would be a producer of value, which is not the case with immaterial labor, which is characterized precisely by the formation of activities (which are not

---

[49] Postone, "Necessity, Labor, and Time," 747-8.
[50] Marx, *Grundrisse*, 705.

always remunerated) and which are presented in the market even as non-labor. The third question concerns the use of the concept of *general intellect,* which refers to the possibility that Marx presents of the constitution of a social individual, source of the general productivity of society. From the latter, the theorists of the immaterial deduce that this is already constituted in the form of a mass intelligentsia that resists being appropriated by capital.[51]

The problems that may develop out of the *Grundrisse,* therefore, are equally political in nature. Problems that run through the entire history of Marxism throughout the 20th century. The problem of the advancement of the productive forces, and of the role of science and technology in capitalist production, raises two issues that are still widely discussed among Marxist authors: the one related to the role of the class struggle and the extensively debated question about the centrality of labor. It should be noted that such importance is placed by some currents of Marxist theory, because in other theoretical perspectives, also analyzed here, what we can call the productivist model is not even in question anymore, nor are such questions posed as fundamental for the current historical moment.

On the first of these questions, class conflict, we are faced with a problem that the authors of the immaterial that we have emphasized throughout this book cannot escape. One of the theses that unfolds, for example, by Antonio Negri, and that we mentioned earlier, is that the validity of immaterial labor in the current phase of capitalism is leading us to a communism of knowledge, which would already be formed nowadays. In this case, although the author continues to speak of social classes,[52] his understanding is that immaterial labor, as a result of the advance of productive forces, represents by its very existence the exhaustion of the mode of production capitalist, however, his concept of communism is, it seems to us, quite strange to what Marx thought.[53]

---

[51]These questions perhaps deserve a separate chapter, but they have already been addressed extensively, mainly in the Marxist literature on the immaterial. It is known that the problem of productive and unproductive labor appears explicitly in chapter VI of *Capital.* In our understanding, succinctly in the face of a complex issue, for Marx, labor that produces surplus value, whether material or immaterial, is productive. If a service produces surplus value, it is productive, even if it is immaterial. But for Marx not all services are. On the second question mentioned, about wage labor, we will return to it later and at different times in this book. This is the distinction between the production of wealth and the production of value. See: Marx, *Capital* chapter VI, 108-20.

[52] Maurizio Lazzarato and Antonio Negri, *Trabalho Imaterial,* 78.

[53] Antonio Negri, *Marx beyond Marx. Lessons on the Grundrisse* (New York: Autonomedia/Pluto, 1991), 165.

The so-called appeasement of the class struggle has been diagnosed since the first quarter of the 20th century, including by some of Marx's followers. The theorists of the Frankfurt School already defended this position at the end of the 1930s, at the same time that the innumerable thinkers that theorize the new social movements, during the last twenty-five years, have insistently pointed to the fact that the opposition between classes is no longer the conflictive epicenter of capitalism. It does not seem to us that Negri, Hardt or Gorz deny the existence of social classes, they only converge to the diagnosis that the processes of social domination must today be understood through other categories.

What we mean is that, according to our interpretation, Marx's work cannot be apprehended as a univocal whole, as a closed system in which all the categories of the critique of political economy would be applied without further to the course of history, and even of the capitalism. This would be the abandonment of dialectics, which is a position explicitly taken by some authors that we will analyze next.[54] It can be said that the emphasis on certain aspects of Marxian thought, to the exclusion of others, demarcated the entire trajectory of Western Marxism and even of contemporary social theory. What seems significant, from the point of view of a critical theory of society, is to apprehend those categories of Marxian thought that are still capable of clarifying and contributing to the understanding and transformation of the present state.

The other issue, exhaustively debated by scholars of the Sociology of Work, concerns the question of the centrality of labor in a post-industrial society. The basic argument in favor of the idea of the centrality of labor starts from an ontological apprehension of Marx's thought, seeing its true expression there. As an ontological argument, that is, of unveiling the social being through the category of labor, this premise leads to the conclusion that the epicenter of human life in society has always been the metabolism between man and nature through labor. This notion argues, therefore, that even in a post-industrial society, or one of late modernity, we will always, necessarily, start from the category of labor as the fundamental nucleus of the constitution of humanity itself. And in the face of the advance of a society founded on immaterial labor, although almost no defender of this position shares the category of the immaterial as relevant to sociological discourse, there will always be, to speak almost metaphorically, the human

---

[54]As for privileging certain aspects of Marxian critique, we refer, for example, to the very form of apprehension that marked the Critical Theory since its beginning. As for the refusal of dialectics, we will see that this position is explicit in the authors of *Multitudes,* and even in Gorz.

being as the one who constitutes the machines and makes possible machines their existence, that is, labor is identified with the very idea of humanity.

In the following pages we will try to clarify how the concept of immaterial labor arises. From what we have seen so far, even in the *Grundrisse* this concept does not occupy a leading role in the Marxian critique of capitalism, but it was in this work that for the first time, within the scope of modern social theory, the idea of the immaterial emerges as a possibility that was already placed in the plan for the development of productive forces. We will see that what today is called immaterial labor will only emerge as a relevant historical phenomenon for the development of capitalism more than a hundred years after the Marxian text. Nevertheless, the reflection on the so-called immaterial labor is part of an even broader and substantive debate regarding the mutations of the capitalist mode of production, the problem about labor time and non-labor time in the production of capitalist value and wealth.

The arguments referring to the end of the production paradigm are already well-known and will reappear in other moments of the argument. For now, it is only worth insisting on the fact that the theoretical wealth of the *Grundrisse* has not yet been fully explored by recent social theory, and the problems suggested there go beyond the field of Marxism itself. In the following pages we will analyze the way in which authors with a recent theoretical production depart from this work to propose a new look at the history of capitalism.

CHAPTER 2

THE ADVENT OF THE IMMATERIAL
AND ITS PROPONENTS

After the initial statements about how the development of the theory of value develops in the *Grundrisse*, constituting a starting point to talk about the concept of the immaterial, it is necessary that we clarify it. Marx wrote the *Grundrisse* more than a century before the immaterial emerged as a central feature of capitalism. Therefore, we understand that Marx did not directly address what we now call immaterial labor but foresaw its emergence as one of the probable historical developments of capitalism, something immanent in the very development of productive forces. Two small books can serve as references for the attempt to explain what immaterial labor is: the set of essays by Negri and Lazzarato published in Brazil under the title *Trabalho Imaterial* and the book *O Imaterial* by André Gorz.

Despite different existing characterizations for advanced capitalism, contemporary social theory, in different theoretical models, usually approaches 20th century capitalism through explanations of the historical significance of Taylorism and Fordism as models of industrial production, and also of society, which represented the hegemonic patterns of wealth production for more than half of the century.[55] The Fordist model of production had as its basic characteristics the production of homogenized and large-scale consumer goods, the vertical organization of labor and its rationally compartmentalized division within the factories, and the use of low-skilled labor. As Harvey says:

> What was special about Ford (and what ultimately distinguished Fordism from Taylorism) was his vision, his explicit recognition that mass production meant mass consumption, a new system of reproduction of labor power, a new politics of control and management of work, a new aesthetics,

---

[55] See, for example: Krishan Kumar, *Da Sociedade Pós-Industrial à Pós-Moderna* (Rio de Janeiro: Jorge Zahar, 1997).

and a new psychology, in short, a new type of democratic, rationalized, modernist and populist society.[56]

The Fordist productive model, characteristic of a capitalism based on industrial production, would reach its limit in the early 1970s, with the advent of a new transformation in capitalism, which it has been designated by some currents of sociology from then on as the advent of post-industrial society, homonymous expression to the well-known book by Daniel Bell first published in 1973.[57] Bell's social theory seeks to indicate the end of a historical phase based on the material production of consumer goods and the Fordist organization of the labor process, implying changes in contemporary society that will find a correspondence a few years later in the notion of post-modernity. For him, in this new stage of society, the sphere of consumption takes precedence over the material production of goods, while the service sector points to a new center of labor relations. In the 1999 preface to his work, Bell presents updated statistical data[58] about the professional occupations of North American workers and developed capitalist countries, showing that most wage workers are currently in this sector. Added to this context is the technological and informational revolution, the advancement of communications, research, and scientific knowledge.[59] As Bell stated in the 1976 *Foreword* of his book:

> The two large dimensions of a post-industrial society, as they are elaborated in this book, are the centrality of theoretical knowledge and the expansion of the service sector as against a manufacturing economy. The first means an increasing dependence on science as the means of innovating and organizing technological change. Most of the industrial societies are highly sensitive to the need for access to scientific knowledge, the organization of research, and the increasing importance of information as the strategic resource in the society.[60]

Although not shared by Bell, other designations emerged for the post-Fordist society, such as consumer society, services, information, network society and many others. With emphases that can be theoretically quite

---

[56] David Harvey, *Condição Pós-Moderna. Uma Pesquisa sobre as origens da mudança cultural* (São Paulo: Loyola, 1993), 121.

[57] Bell, *The Coming of Post-Industrial Society*.

[58] We refer to the fact that in the original edition of his book (1973) the author presented data collected mainly in the second half of the 1960s. In the edition mentioned above, Bell presents statistical data collected more than two decades later in order to reinforce the arguments of his initial thesis.

[59] We will return to Bell especially from chapter 4 of this book.

[60] Bell, *The Coming of Post-Industrial Society*, xcvii.

different, all these designations seem to point to the same historical phenomenon, characterized by a significant expansion of the spheres of consumption, services and the role of information. In some cases, such changes come to be understood as the emergence of a new mode of production, such is the degree of change that has taken place in capitalist economic relations in recent decades.[61] We have even more audacious cases, such as Rifkin who points out a trend from the beginning of the 20th century regarding the end of capitalism in what has most substantially characterized it historically, at least in his understanding, which is private property and material labor, manifesting the entry into what he calls cultural capitalism.

Surprisingly, Bell's neoconservative theses,[62] in which the roles of information and knowledge in the new stage of society are highlighted, find resonance in theoretical traditions radically opposed to his. This is the case of the heirs of "Italian workerism" Antonio Negri and Maurizio Lazzarato, who depart directly from the Marxian work to affirm, like Bell, that society has become fundamentally post-industrial.[63]

We understand that Negri, Hardt and Lazzarato defend almost identical positions regarding the concept of the immaterial, while the similarities between them and Gorz are less in the face of a series of differentiated positions, both in the political and epistemological aspects, that is, they have very theoretical positions distinct, although, on the other hand, we also find some similarities between them. The definition of immaterial labor is already a first problem for its proponents. According to Lazzarato:

> The concept of immaterial labor refers to *two different aspects* of labor. On the one hand, as regards the "informational content" of the commodity, it refers directly to the changes taking place in workers' labor processes in big

---

[61] See, for example: Moulier-Boutang, *Le Capitalisme Cognitif.*

[62] About the "conservatism" of Bell, see Jürgen Habermas, "Modernidade – Um Projeto Inacabado," in *Um Ponto Cego no Projeto Moderno de Jürgen Habermas*, ed. Otília Fiori Arantes e Paulo Eduardo Arantes (São Paulo: Brasiliense, 1992), 107.

[63] Despite this similarity, we will also see how this privilege of knowledge and information will acquire different contours among these authors. As for the fact that Antonio Negri's thought has its genesis in the 1960s with the so-called Italian workerism, this is something that has already been mentioned several times in recent sociological literature. In the introduction to the book by Negri *Marx beyond Marx* there is an exposition by Maurizio Viano that explores the initial formation of the Italian thinker and in the classic labor of Mario Tronti there is a long afterword by Yann Moulier-Boutang on the history and the theses of Italian workerism. See: Mario Tronti, *Operários e Capital* (Porto: Afrontamento, 1976).

companies in the industrial and tertiary sectors, where the skills involved in direct labor are increasingly skills involving cybernetics and computer control (...) On the other hand, as regards the activity that produces the "cultural content" of the commodity, immaterial labor involves a series of activities that are not normally recognized as "work" – in other words, the kinds of activities involved in defining and fixing cultural and artistic standards, fashions, tastes, consumer norms, and, more strategically, public opinion.[64]

Antonio Negri, whose theoretical production is very strongly associated with Maurizio Lazzarato and Michael Hardt, can be seen as one of the main thinkers in recent social theory dealing with the meaning of immaterial labor and its status in the configuration of Western societies at the beginning of this century. Negri is among those who intend to understand the current stage of capitalism from the category of immaterial labor, with reference to Marx's *Grundrisse*. Although he devoted an entire book to this work by Marx,[65] his specific theoretical approaches to immaterial labor are not very rigorous in terms of the definition of this category. The theses developed by Negri and Lazzarato in the set of essays mentioned above are, when it comes to the immaterial, the same ones developed by Hardt and Negri in *Empire*[66] or *O Trabalho de Dionísio*,[67] although in the latter we see the reading of the authors about what we could call the postmodern political condition.

Negri's work consolidates the view that industrial production has become post-industrial, a post-Taylorist production, where the production of services, labor relations and human relations themselves as a whole – human subjectivity – are in the contemporary society based primarily on communication processes, which is the new basis of social wealth.[68] But the way he defines the immaterial is clearly presented, especially when he identifies it with services, which curiously brings him closer to Daniel Bell's theses. According to Hardt and Negri:

---

[64] Maurizio Lazzarato, "Immaterial Labor." In *Radical Thought in Italy*, edited by Paolo Virno and Michael Hardt (Minneapolis: University of Minnesota Press, 1996), 133.

[65] Negri, *Marx Beyond Marx*.

[66] Michael Hardt and Antonio Negri, *Empire* (Cambridge: Harvard University Press, 2000).

[67] Michael Hardt e Antonio Negri, *O Trabalho de Dionísio* (Juiz de Fora: UFJF-Pazulin, 2004).

[68] By placing the concept of communication as the epicenter of the new capitalist relations, they converge with the Habermasian thesis regarding the end of the production paradigm. On the other hand, the theorization of immaterial labor maintains the centrality of the category "labor" in the understanding of capitalist society, although it is no longer about wage labor that produces commodities.

> Since the production of services result in no material and durable good, we
> define the labor involved in this production as *immaterial labor* – that is,
> labor that produces an immaterial good, such as a service, cultural product,
> knowledge, or communication.[69]

If we take the sentence above as a definition sketch by Negri, the
immaterial presents itself as capable of four distinct meanings: service;
cultural product; knowledge; and information. One of our arguments, to be
presented later, is that these authors do not very clearly explain this so-called
"cultural product". We can no longer say the same about the communicational
and informational aspects that configure the immaterial, as well as its
identification with services.

The issue of services as an expression of immaterial labor is not
something easy, as we can assume that not every type of service is expressed
as immaterial labor. On the other hand, we enter the question about the role
of services in capitalist production as a whole. In addition to the fact that for
Negri, Hardt and Lazzarato we live today in a new mode of production, the
services category is central in their attempt to tell us what the immaterial is:

> In short, we can distinguish three types of immaterial labor that drive the
> service sector at the top of the informational economy. The first is involved
> in industrial production that has been informationalized and has incorporated
> communication technology in a way that transforms the production process
> itself. Manufacturing is regarded as a service and the material labor of the
> production of durable goods mixes with and tends toward immaterial labor.
> Second is the immaterial labor of analytic and symbolic tasks, which itself
> breakdown into creative and intelligent manipulation on the one hand and
> routine symbolic tasks on the other. Finally, the third type of immaterial
> labor involves the production and manipulation of affect and requires
> (virtual or real) human contact, labor in the bodily mode. These are the three
> types of labor that drive the postmodernization of the global economy.[70]

For Negri, in the present phase of capitalism, the changes we have seen
refer primarily to the very concept of labor power and its role in the
production process. We would be facing a situation in which the appropriation
of other people's labor time is no longer the basis for sustaining capitalist
wealth, an argument that is in line with our initial exposition on the
Grundrisse. We can even say that his conception is near to that of Habermas
about science and technology as the main productive forces,[71] but for Negri

---

[69] Hardt and Negri, *Empire*, 290.

[70] Ibid., 293.

[71] See: Jürgen Habermas, *Técnica e Ciência Enquanto Ideologia* (São Paulo: Abril
Cultural, 1983).

communication does not point to the same Habermasian conceptual status. Intersubjectivity, in the sense of communicative action, does not appear as a new epistemological model, even because, following some formulations from Deleuze and Foucault, their theorization of the immaterial and the mutation in the productive forces emphasizes the category of subjectivity in its constitution.[72] Unlike Habermas and Honneth, informed by the young Hegel's theory of intersubjectivity, Hardt, Negri and Lazzarato make use of a third phase of Foucauldian thought.[73] For them, the subjectivity that accompanies the immaterial no longer refers to a disciplinary society, but to the society of control, which is the inflection point for understanding the relationship between subjectivity and immaterial labor as something that concerns the concept of biopower:

> Second, Foucault's work allows us to recognize the *biopolitical* nature of the new paradigm of power. Biopower is the form of power that regulates social life from its interior, following it, interpreting it, absorbing it, and rearticulating it. Power can achieve an effective command over the entire life of the population when it becomes an integral, vital function that all individuals embrace and reactivates of his or her own accord.[74]

Considering characteristics also pointed out by post-Fordism theorists regarding immaterial production, we see, according to Negri and Lazzarato, that factory production now occurs in a more decentralized way, where the various stages of production no longer occur in a single physical place, which characterized large-scale industry in Fordism. There is a broad process of outsourcing the various stages of production, that is, to produce a good or a commodity, industries make use of countless other companies that provide a service to them, reducing activities located in their own place to the minimum necessary for the production.

The authors converge, to a considerable extent, to approaches that deal with the so-called productive restructuring, a recurring theme in the Sociology of Work. Authors who approach this theme also point out the political aspects of post-Fordism, such as the deregulation of labor laws, new forms of management and the mythologizing of the idea of total

---

[72] Which leads us to state that, as an epistemological model, its election of communication as a privileged point for analyzing the world of labor itself does not imply an adherence to the communication paradigm in the sense of linguistic pragmatics.

[73] Negri, Hardt and Lazzarato refer to the last Foucault, already present in the book *History of Sexuality*. His theses on the society of control owe much more, however, to Gilles Deleuze.

[74] Hardt and Negri, *Empire*, 23-4.

quality.[75] Such modifications, with emphases that are sometimes a little different from those we are dealing with here, refer to the same historical phenomenon.

In Negri and Lazzarato's view, for commodities, whether material or immaterial, to be shown as a result of the production process, the role of information and cooperation at labor becomes central. The worker can no longer perform his tasks mechanically and in isolation (as happened with the mass worker) but must deal with a multiplicity of functions that require creativity, initiative, differentiated knowledge, communication, and cooperation skills. The set of such characteristics pertinent to the productive process, and which concern a greater intellectual qualification of the worker, is like those characterizations made by Marx, called *general intellect.* This makes it possible, in Negri's view, to conceive that the advent of immaterial labor corresponds to the formation of a mass intellectuality, which in turn would also be the starting point for thinking about both domination and human emancipation in the present conditions. Lazzarato and Negri takes up the Marxian text:

> In this transformation, it is neither the immediate work performed by the man himself, nor the time he works, but the appropriation of his general productivity, his understanding of nature and the mastery over it through his existence as a social body – in other words, it is the development of the social individual that presents itself as the great pillar of support for production and wealth. *The theft of someone else's time, on whom the current wealth* is based presents itself as a miserable base in relation to this new base that has developed and that was created by the industry itself.[76]

Another characteristic, also emphasized by other authors, refers to the fact that an increasing number of industries reduce their stocks to a minimum standard, inverting the productive logic; first, the sale of the commodity is conducted, and increasingly through mechanisms such as the internet and teleshopping, and only after this determination of consumption is its material production carried out. Furthermore, contrary to Fordist production, there would no longer be a complete standardization of consumer goods, but these would depend directly on the variable and fragmentary interests dictated by the consumer. Hardt and Negri rely on

---

[75] See : Jaques Bidet et Jacques Texier (Eds.). *La crise du travail* (Paris: Presses Universitaires de France, 1995).

[76] The authors refer to the Italian edition of the Karl Marx, *Grundrisse or Lineamenti fondamentali della critica dell'economia politica* (Florence: La Nuova Itália, 1978), 401-2. Citation apud Lazzarato and Negri, *Trabalho Imaterial*, 28.

Toyotism itself to develop their conception of the relationship between production and consumption:

> Toyotism is based on an inversion of the Fordist structure of communication between production and consumption. Ideally, according to this model, production planning will communicate with markets constantly and immediately. Factories keep zero inventories, and commodities will be produced just in time, according to the present demand of the existing markets [...] but an inversion of the relationship because, at least in theory, the production decision actually comes after and in reaction to the market decision.[77]

We are facing a thesis whose theoretical consequences need to be considered in their entirety. The fact that today an increasing number of companies control their productive structure in a different way from what happened under Fordism is not the same as saying, as Negri does, that today the capitalist production process takes place primarily in the sphere of consumption. If Negri is right, we would no longer be talking about the capitalist mode of production in the same sense in which Marx understands, insofar as for Marx production, distribution and consumption were constituted in moments of the same process, whose totality was achieved with the very concept of capitalism:

> The "laws and conditions" of the production of wealth and the laws of the "distribution of wealth" are the same laws in different forms, and both changes, undergo the same historic process; are as such only moments of a historic process.[78]

For Negri, Hardt and Lazzarato, the so-called new mode of production would thus be a primacy of consumption over production, eliminating the kind of distinction made by Marx between production, circulation, and consumption. Conceptions such as Bell's post-industrial society and Baudrillard's consumer society also pose problems regarding the understanding of the relationship between production and consumption in a phase of advanced capitalism. This shift to the sphere of consumption should not surprise us in the face of the fact that several of these authors, under the strong influence of post-structuralism, began to question the very adequacy of a critique of political economy as a privileged form of critique for understanding the current historic transformations. Towards Baudrillard, for example, his concepts of seduction, desire and hyper-reality refer much

---

[77] Hardt and Negri, *Empire*, 290.
[78] Marx, *Grundrisse*, 832.

more to a type of political economy of the sign, than to the categories of Marxian origin. In the case of *Multitudes theorists,* such as Lazzarato, although the use of political economy concepts is still evident, their theoretical perspective has shown a great effort to reread Gabriel Tarde as a thinker capable of illuminating the current stage of contemporary society, and more recently, the author has resorted to the modern Leibnizian idea of "monads" to re-elaborate it in the form of a neo-monadology:

> I intend to approach the interpretation of the process of constitution of the *socius* from a particular perspective: the double critique of individualism and holism undertaken by Tarde, and the new concept of cooperation that he suggests. This concept of cooperation is radically different from what we find in the works of Adam Smith and Marx: it is about cooperation of the multiplicity of monads, based on the modalities of creation and effectuation of possible worlds *versus* cooperation as a division of labor, following the modalities of production or praxis.[79]

Negri and Lazzarato emphasize that there is a need for an increasing mobilization of companies to apprehend the taste of consumers as quickly as possible. Taste, of course, leads us to the problem of the relationship between aesthetics and capitalism. Once again, the influence of Deleuze and post-structuralism appears for Negri, insofar as the neo-Nietzschean conception of desire as something productive also unfolds. The immateriality of labor is also present in the very formation of this taste as it is through marketing, advertising, and effective use of the media that the economy of the immaterial becomes a producer of wealth. Trends related to customs, behaviors and even values become cultural and subjective prerequisites for production, perhaps its main characteristic. Both the sphere of those who produce and that of consumption are thus subsumed under immaterial labor. Labor activities guided by information also appear as a central aspect in obtaining profit, since the entire production circuit will depend on such information, including those related to the taste of the consumer public.

With a different theoretical contribution from this, André Gorz also undertakes an interpretation of capitalism in its current phase where immaterial labor plays a key role in his critique of society. In Gorz's view, in addition to a trend towards hegemony of the service sector, capitalism has as a fundamental characteristic an immateriality of labor embodied in the role of *savoir,* knowledge and information, and similarly to Negri and the theorists of *Multitudes,* for him, the intellectual capacity of individuals comes to occupy a privileged position in labor relationships of a new type.

---

[79] Maurizio Lazzarato, *As Revoluções do Capitalismo* (Rio de Janeiro: Civilização Brasileira, 2007), 28.

Gorz's conception of the immaterial converges to the notion of cognitive capitalism, that is, to the construction of a theory about human capital as the key element for understanding labor relations in the current stage of capitalism.[80] The worker of the immaterial age tends to be a kind of "entrepreneur of himself", whose participation in the market is dependent on investments and qualifications that are increasingly intellectualized and symbolic. In the immaterial production of wealth, not only science and technology, but knowledge and *savoir* conceived more broadly, are postulated as the main productive forces. Faced with those who defend the centrality of labor in the constitution of capitalism, Gorz presents, as Postone had done, a position that moves from an anthropological approach to human labor to situate it as a historical and analytical problematic, implying this position both in a confluence as in a critique of Marxian thought itself. It is in this way that labor, as a specific manifestation of human action, must be understood primarily in the historical developmental milestones of modern industrial society, which, in turn, can only have its full sociological elucidation when inseparable from the understanding of the importance of rationality in its constitution.

Epicenter of Marx's emancipatory project and social theory, the proletariat loses in this historical period, in Gorz's view, not only its status as a collective subject necessarily destined to revolutionize the relations of production, as possible the transformative consciousness of the working class, but it also became difficult to identify the proletariat itself as a structurally identifiable class in capitalist economic relations.[81]

Marx conceived human labor, in his first works, as the ontological nucleus through which we apprehend not only the realm of necessity and the processes of domination, but also as the starting point for thinking about human emancipation and freedom. Gorz, in an analogous way to Hannah Arendt, shows us that all labor with an economic purpose is characterized by a specific form of rationality, always focused, within the framework of

---

[80] Gorz is concerned throughout his work with understanding the category of labor. His positions, however, will change throughout his intellectual biography. We understand that it is possible to identify a phase that goes up to *Adeus ao Proletariado* and, starting with it, lasts more than two decades. However, the book *O Imaterial* breaks with aspects of Gorz's thought that were present. Even so, we identify a certain unity in his thinking. See: Sílvio Camargo, "Capitalism and Utopia in The Social Theory of André Gorz." *New Proposals: Journal of Marxism and Interdisciplinary Inquiry*, 11, no.1 (Summer 2020): 59-65.

[81] See: André Gorz, *Adeus ao Proletariado* (Rio de Janeiro: Forense Universitária, 1987).

capitalism, towards the market or exchange value.[82] This means that all labor with an economic purpose is destined for heteronomy. It would no longer be enough, therefore, to think of human emancipation only as the abolition of private ownership of the means of production and construction of a socialist society guided by the collective appropriation of such means. Human emancipation, for Gorz, involves the abolition of labor itself as the articulating ground of human sociability.

The phenomenon of alienation is no longer understood only as the contradiction inherent in the process of wage labor, but heteronomy refers to the type of rationalization that accompanies labor with an economic purpose, whether waged or not. For Gorz there is a complete antinomy between labor and autonomy, and the latter can only be found in activities that take place outside this rationality. In our understanding, Gorz approaches the central theses that guided the Critical Theory, that is, the critique of the inseparability between rationality, modernity, and domination. With a discourse more focused on the Sociology of Work, Gorz insists on the urgent need to understand the role of labor in the mutation of capitalism, and, on the need, based on this understanding, to rethink the dimension of utopia in terms distinct from those of traditional Marxism.[83]

Gorz's thesis of economic rationalization seeks to show us that it is labor itself, whenever supported by an economic purpose, which engenders the limitation of individuals' freedom. A free society involves the abolition of labor itself, or, more easily, its gradual reduction, until human beings can produce their lives through a different rationality. We will see later how the utopian elements of Gorz's thought are directly dependent on this conception of a heteronomous rationality that accompanies labor in modernity. In an analogous way to the arguments presented by Moishe Postone, we can say that for Gorz a change in the mode of distribution of wealth does not alter the substratum of domination that is rooted in the very form of labor in modernity.

Like Marcuse, Postone and Negri, Gorz will also look to the *Grundrisse* for elements of a critique of capitalism that in various aspects would have anticipated current trends in capitalism. At the same time, he acquires a new proportion in his work, a certain type of reflection on temporality that unfolds both in a questioning of the Marxian theory of value-labor, but also goes beyond it. On the one hand, with regard to the critique of political economy, Gorz investigates the way in which time is the condition for the creation of value and wealth, but on the other hand, time as something that

---

[82] About the economic rationality see: André Gorz, *Metamorfoses do Trabalho* (São Paulo: Annablume, 2003).

[83] See, for example: André Gorz, *Paths to Paradise* (Boston: South and Press, 1985).

also refers to the scope of human actions in a spectrum of experiences that are equally constitutive of capitalism. Human actions that take place outside of experience and labor time are situated in what Gorz and Habermas call the lifeworld (*Lebenswelt*).

When explaining a theory guided by a dual vision of society, Gorz establishes that the labor time, like the time that the workers spend inside the factory, is the measure not only of the creation of value, as it is clear in the Marxian thought, but it is also which makes the heteronomy of workers possible. Since his work *Adeus ao Proletariado*, Gorz starts to defend that emancipation is no longer a liberation at labor, but a liberation from labor. The rupture of that process that Marx and Gorz himself saw as alienation can no longer be achieved with labor time as a starting point, but with non-labor time, as well as labor that can no longer be measured in time.[84]

Time is treated not only as a *locus* of value production, as a category relevant to the critique of political economy, but it is also dimensioned as a philosophical category, as a parameter through which human existence itself is thought. For Gorz, labor time is what imprisons, and free time is what opens up countless possibilities for a life endowed with meaning. Non-labor time is related to leisure activities or even labor activities that are not intended to create value. Just as Marx in *The German Ideology* had alluded to the possibilities that arise in a society that would break with the capitalist division of labor,[85] Gorz maintains that a future society capable of enabling autonomy will have to provide individuals with an increased possibility of non-labor.

As for Habermas, these non-labor experiences take place in the lifeworld. But, unlike Habermas, this lifeworld is not that sphere of action in which spontaneous interactions take place based on the solidity of normative patterns, but the time and space of life in which social integration, as opposed to functional integration, takes place; it is mediated by the conflict between individual behaviors and institutionalized norms.[86] The conflictive dimension of the lifeworld, the estrangement of the individual in relation to his own tradition, manifests the phenomenologically apprehensible dimension of this lifeworld, expressing some intellectual influences that have always guided Gorz's thinking, especially Sartre.

Temporality is fundamental to understanding immaterial labor. For Gorz, immaterial labor is increasingly replacing the material production of goods and commodities, causing the entire scope of the critique of Marxian political economy, the theory of value, to be questioned at its fundamental

---

[84] Gorz, *O Imaterial*, 25.
[85] Marx and Engels, *The German Ideology*, 52-3.
[86] Gorz, *Metamorfoses do Trabalho*, 172.

core, precisely labor time as the constitutive basis of value. Immaterial labor represents the set of activities, both industrial and services, marked by cooperation, communication, and intellectual activities, which have knowledge as their fundamental basis.

According to Gorz, we are in a phase of capitalism in which knowledge is the central element of production: "in the knowledge economy, all labor, whether in industrial production or in the service sector, contains a component of knowledge whose importance is increasing."[87] In the framework of a phase of economic development that other authors also call post-industrial society, cognitive capitalism imposes changes primarily on the category of labor itself: "Under these conditions, labor, which since Adam Smith has been taken as a substance of value common to all commodities is no longer measurable in units of time."[88]

The phase of capitalism to which immaterial labor corresponds results from an exacerbation of economic rationality, notably with regard to technological advancement, which leads to the limit situation of putting the very concept of "human" in check. In a capitalism no longer centered on industrial production and the appropriation of labor time, the processes of computerization and technological development go hand in hand with a dematerialization of society:

> Capitalism has largely dematerialized the main productive forces: labor (and we are only at the beginning of this process) and fixed capital. The most important form of fixed capital is henceforth stagnant knowledge instantly available through information technologies, and the most important form of workforce is intellect.[89]

Knowledge and *savoir* become the central aspect in the production of capitalist wealth, where immaterial capital is rapidly replacing material fixed capital, as was already announced in the passages of the *Grundrisse* mentioned above. From the outset, however, it is necessary to point out that the terms knowledge and *savoir* have different meanings for Gorz, and such a distinction will be fundamental to understand all the arguments that involve immaterial labor. For Gorz, knowledge refers to formal learning and qualifications, such as those that individuals learn in universities or research centers, while *savoir* refers more directly to the *Lebenswelt itself*, to everyday, spontaneous, non-formal learning, not necessarily formalizable. And it is

---

[87] Gorz, *O Imaterial*, 9.
[88] Ibid.
[89] André Gorz, *Misérias do Presente, Riqueza do Possível* (São Paulo: Annablume, 2004a), 13.

the importance of this *savoir* in the new capitalist relations that is shown as a peculiarity of immaterial labor:

> *Savoir* is above all a practical capacity, a competence that does not necessarily imply formalizable, codifiable knowledge. Most body *savoirs* escapes the possibility of formalization. They are not taught; we learn them through practice, through custom, that is, when someone exercises themselves doing what it is about learning to do.[90]

A fundamental change concerns the very status of capitalist domination at this stage, as it is no longer focused exclusively on the modern figure of wage labor, giving way to a preeminence of human capital. Here, we no longer deal with the worker who sells his workforce and finds himself alienated in this process, but with the worker who must acquire a set of *savoirs* and skills that refer to his own daily life, that is, to qualifications that they concern not only labor time, but knowledge that now encompasses non-labor time, free time.

The use of intelligence, the exponent par excellence of the immateriality of labor, becomes the key element both for industrial production procedures,[91] as well as for other activities that also produce wealth, such as services. But also, a whole multiplicity of activities involved in a capitalist production that depends directly, as at no other time in history, on processes related to consumption activities on the one hand, and on the other, on experiences that refer directly to everyday life, but which represent a new manifestation of capital, the immaterial capital:

> [...] It also indicates that the exchange value of commodities, whether material or not, is no longer ultimately determined by the amount of general social labor they contain, but, above all, by their content of knowledge, information, general intelligences. It is the latter, and no longer abstract social labor measurable according to a single standard, which becomes the main social substance common to all commodities. It becomes the main source of value and profit, and thus, according to several authors, the main form of labor and capital.[92]

We must remember that the Marxian notion of *general intellect* already pointed to a possible exhaustion of the production of value through the labor

---

[90] Gorz, *O Imaterial*, 32.

[91] Lazzarato and Negri, as we have seen before, are quite clear in pointing out the capacities for cooperation, communication, self-organization, initiative, creativity, etc., as determining elements of a new behavior at labor that characterizes post-Fordist industrial production.

[92] Gorz, *O Imaterial*, 31.

time and the *quantity* of labor supplied, insofar as the advance of the productive forces, notably science and technology, would pass, in Marx's own view, to occupy a central position in the productive process. Marx already predicted, therefore, a process of development of capitalism in which knowledge would come to occupy the role of the main productive force:

> With that, production based on exchange value break down, and the direct, material production process is stripped of the form of penury and antithesis. The free development of individualities and hence not the reduction of necessary labour time so as to posit surplus labour, but rather the general reduction of the necessary of society to a minimum, which then corresponds to the artistic scientific, etc. development of the individuals in the time set free, and with the means created, for all of them.[93]

This notion of *general intellect* as a key category for understanding the current phase of capitalism is one of the points of approximation between Gorz's theses and those of Negri and Lazzarato. Underlying it is the understanding that today there is a general productivity, not materially apprehensible, which is placed by the accumulation of knowledge and *savoir* that became the inflection point of capitalist productivity. This general productivity, which is a general *savoir* that expands to the whole of society, at the same time that it is a producer of wealth, is also potentially resistant to private appropriation. It is, in fact, for Negri, a communist potential, insofar as it goes against the individualizing and privatizing logic of capitalism. This is how the Marxian *general intellect* would reappear in advanced capitalism as a potency for a new type of utopia, or as the main basis through which capitalism creates in its development at the same time its limit of existence.

Free time, the cultural and everyday experiences that form the so-called lifeworld, are also producers of a certain type of value or wealth. This means, according to one of our hypotheses, that in this free time what Gorz calls economic rationality will also be imposed, contrary to the idea of a communism of knowledge that is gestated in it. This optimism about the impossibility of *savoir* to become privately appropriated is one of the main points of approximation between Negri and Gorz, but it is also shared by most authors who relate the category of immaterial labor to the concept of cognitive capitalism.[94] On the other hand, they also have different understandings of society and capitalism, especially with regard to problems

---

[93] Marx, *Grundrisse*, 705-6.
[94] See, for example: Moulier-Boutang, *Le Capitalisme Cognitif* and Christian Azaïs, Antonella Corsani, and Patrick Dieuaide, eds, *Vers un capitalisme cognitif.*

of a political and normative dimension. Although the *Grundrisse* are the starting point for both to reach the same conclusion about the centrality of immaterial labor within a new configuration of capitalism, their understanding of the processes of sociability differs in terms of the epistemological influences they deal with; while Gorz seeks to bring Marxism closer to Weber and phenomenology, Negri seeks to bring it closer to French post-structuralism.

So far, we have tried to sketch what immaterial labor is, starting mainly from its two most prominent representatives in this first decade of the 21st century. We are trying to show that from these authors, and from their reading of Marx's *Grundrisse*, the hypothesis is revealed that the stage of capitalism that began about three decades ago has as its main characteristic the emergence of immaterial labor. The hypothesis around the centrality of the immaterial, however, seems to meet strong resistance from those that we will call here, without any pejorative connotation, traditional Marxism. On the other hand, the critique of the ontological approach to labor, the emphasis on the role of science and technology in the process of capitalist accumulation and the attempt to understand capitalist domination not only as class domination, find resonance in the Critical Theory of the Frankfurt School.

Our purpose, in the pages that follow, is to seek to understand the current transformations taking place in world capitalism in the light of the category of immaterial labor, and even more precisely, to try to understand how the forms of social domination engendered by modernity find themselves in the present stage a completely different moment in relation to previous stages in the history of capitalism. In this way, it will also be necessary to explain from which theoretical bases we undertake this critique of domination, and then to explain how to relate it to those authors treated so far.

CHAPTER 3

CRITICAL THEORY AND LATE CAPITALISM

In the two preceding chapters, we set out the thesis about immaterial labor, by adopting the *Grundrisse* as a privileged starting point, as well as the central ideas of the authors who, in our understanding, were the protagonists of the ongoing debate about the immaterial. The problem that we now pose is how to think about the very concept of capitalism based on the thesis regarding the prominence of immaterial labor. Our understanding is that the concept of late capitalism, initiated by the Frankfurt School, can contribute to the elucidation of the historical conditions in progress, provided that, at the same time, we can offer a contribution to the very redefinition of this concept, as the historical conditions in which it was coined are radically changing.

The term late capitalism has historically had different theoretical elaborations, from the first generation of Frankfurtians, through Habermas, and more emphatically in the works of Mandel[95] and Jameson.[96] The work of the latter, whom we consider an heir of the critical theory of society, is the one that is closest to the understanding of capitalism that we are going to present. However, its definition of capitalism, on the one hand, has some inaccuracies, and on the other, it does not envision the centrality of immaterial labor for contemporary forms of wealth production. In our view, Jameson's theses on late capitalism are decisive for the elucidation of the relationship between culture and economy in advanced capitalism, but they are insufficient, as it was historically for the Critical Theory, regarding the problematization of the category of labor in relation to the transformations of contemporary society.

The thinkers of the immaterial that we approached earlier, especially Negri and Gorz, converge on the concept of *cognitive capitalism* as the one that best expresses world capitalism in its current phase, and this will be the subject of the following chapter. For now, our interest is to trace a brief historical genealogy of the concept of late capitalism, understanding that

---

[95] Ernest Mandel, *O Capitalismo Tardio* (São Paulo: Abril Cultural, 1982).
[96] Jameson, *Pós-Modernismo.*

even its original formulations can still contribute to grasp of capitalism in the 21st century. In addition, we intend to present the hypothesis, in this chapter and in the following ones, that a re-elaboration of the concept of late capitalism is necessary from the problematization of immaterial labor. With this, we hope to somehow contribute to an understanding of capitalism from the foundations laid by the critical theory of society.

In recent debates in social theory, those who claim the heritage of Critical Theory have engaged in a deep debate around the concepts of recognition and redistribution, whose most significant landmark is the book by Axel Honneth *Luta por Reconhecimento*.[97] Proposing to develop a moral grammar of social conflicts Honneth and his interlocutors openly place themselves in the field of a post-socialist debate, not only of "real post-socialism," but as having as a presumption the complete overcoming of the terms that guide the discussion within the productivist model. In this case, the debate between the latter goes beyond not only a convincing explanation of the role of labor in the current phase of contemporary society, but also no longer deals with issues related to the accumulation of capital, the production of wealth and the fetishism of commodity.

Our attempt to understand and problematize the notion of immaterial labor has the sense that we also seek to extend to the present moment some of the precepts of Critical Theory, understanding that modern rationality, the so-called instrumental reason, has metamorphosed in the present into more sophisticated manifestations, or less visible, whose objective content is an extension of modern capitalist domination. And in addition to the characteristics indicated above regarding Critical Theory, the critique of capitalist domination seems to us to be the most distinctive feature of what we call the Frankfurt School and one of its greatest legacies.[98] In this sense, we believe that a brief resumption of the characteristics of the critique of capitalism undertaken by Frankfurtians is pertinent, since one of our central arguments has such thinkers as a starting point: the inseparability between culture and economy in the processes of domination of modernity.

The articulation nucleus of the Frankfurt School, since the creation of the *Institute for Social Research*, made reference to several theoretical and historical aspects. One was the need to resist two currents of thought that were influential between the 1920s and 1930s: positivism (with its variables) and Soviet Marxism and III International. In addition, the group inspired by

---

[97] Axel Honneth, *Luta por Reconhecimento*: *A Gramática Moral dos Conflitos Sociais* (São Paulo: Ed. 34, 2003).
[98] About power and domination in Critical Theory see: Axel Honneth, *The Critique of Power. Reflective Stages in a Critical Social Theory* (London: The MIT Press, 1991).

Grossmann and Horkheimer proposed carrying out interdisciplinary research, a task undertaken with relative success, the results of which were published in the *Zeitschrift für Sozialforschung*. This historical moment will also be marked by important debates in the field of critique of political economy, highlighting the problem related to the theory of the collapse and crisis of capitalism.

The Frankfurt School's thought took place from the beginning as a need to understand the transformations in capitalist society, whose manifestations at this historical moment were related to new elements regarding the process of capitalist accumulation. The understanding of these transformations, however, from the beginning went beyond the specific debate of political economy, since the questions about the authoritarian state, and what we can call the subjectivity of the masses, are incorporated into a broader analysis of capitalism. The Frankfurtian view soon learned that the capitalist transformations that matured in the 1920s meant a break with 19th century capitalism and required a reflection on the Marxian categories themselves and their analysis of liberal capitalism.

The expression *late capitalism* marked the entire history of the Frankfurt School and has also been claimed by other thinkers who are affiliated with what we call *Critical Theory*. An expression developed at the end of the decade of the 1930s, the notion of late capitalism served as support for Adorno and Horkheimer until the end of the 1960s in the development of their theory of society. It emerged in the discussions of the *Institute for Social Research* and had as its main exponent Frederick Pollock and his conception of organized capitalism. Although Pollock's theses were not shared by all members of the Institute, such as Grossmann and Neumann, his conception of capitalism influenced, and was shared, both by Adorno and by Horkheimer. Pollock's central thesis was that capitalism at that historical moment ceased to be an economy given over to the free game of the market, having its rules politically managed, and thus becoming an organized capitalism. The political sphere and its configuration of power began to control the course of the accumulation process:

> The term *state capitalism* (so runs the argument) is possibly misleading insofar as it could be understood to denote a society wherein the state is the sole owner of all capital, and this is not necessarily meant by those who use it. Nevertheless, it indicates four items better than do all other suggested items: that state capitalism is the successor of private capitalist; that the state

assumes important functions of the private capitalist; that the profit interests still play a significant role; and that it is not socialism.[99]

In the Adornian version, this form of capitalism found correspondence in his thesis of the administered society. For Adorno, capitalism became late not only as a result of an advance of the productive forces that tended to make society as a whole determined by the dictates of technique, but also converged, as for the other Frankfurtians, to the perception of a new role of the state as regulator of the economy. And parallel to this, the emergence of mass culture and the culture industry. Not only for Pollock and Adorno, but also for Horkheimer and Marcuse, the bureaucratic and administrative control of the economy became evident as a result of the historical context of the affirmation of Nazism and Fascism. The conception of late capitalism that presents itself in this period – between 1937 and 1941 – showed, on the other hand, not only as an economic theory of capitalism, but refers to an apprehension of contemporary society in which, in addition to the participation of political sphere within the scope of the economy, the role of culture and its intertwining with technique will also acquire a singular importance.[100] The transformation of culture into a form of industry, having as main references music and cinema, transformed the reflection on cultural artifacts into something more than the traditional critique of the forms of reproduction of bourgeois ideology.

For Adorno, the notion of late capitalism appears at various times in his work, from the 1940s to the late 1960s. Under the influence of Pollock, Adorno problematizes the expression by pointing out other new characteristics of the capitalist mode of production. Always keeping its conception of "not identity" and totality as philosophical references, the Adornian dialectic perceives in the new stage of capitalism a new type of domination, different from that which marked liberal capitalism, insofar as instrumental rationality now expands to other spheres of human life. In this sense, late capitalism for Adorno is equivalent to the critique of the culture industry, insofar as, in addition to the authoritarian state, this industry appears as the other pole of late-stage capitalism.

With few incursions into properly economic language, the notion of late capitalism is, however, the substrate for a new theory of domination.[101]

---

[99] Frederick Pollock, "State Capitalism: Its Possibilities and Limitations," in *Critical Theory and Society* ed. Stephen Bronner and Douglas Kellner (New York: Routledge, 1989), 96.

[100] About the first years of Frankfurt School, see especially: Martin Jay (*La Imaginación Dialéctica*. Madrid: Taurus, 1986).

[101] Honneth, *The Critique* and Camargo, *Modernidade e Dominação*.

Adorno will emphasize, in texts more focused on sociology, that the new form of domination does not abdicate from the Marxian theory of value and emphasizes that in late capitalism the relations of production are incorporated into the productive forces themselves.[102]

We think that, in addition to the contributions that the first generation of Frankfurtians may have given to the economic debate on capitalism, the great theoretical change that begins with them is the way of understanding the relationship between culture and economy. Adorno's conception of the culture industry will show culture as a central aspect in capitalist production, and the fundamental way in which the bourgeoisie continues to sustain its domination. On the other hand, Adorno's analysis of capitalism does not propose a clear attempt to criticize the category of labor and its real expression on the so-called "shop floor", but taking as a presupposition the domination existing there, seeks to understand its extension beyond of labor time. This beyond labor time, or non-labor time, with the contemporary advance of capitalism, will extend the process of reification to the whole of the worker's lifetime. Instrumental rationality, the central core of late capitalism, leaves the economic-productive sphere and creates a productive structure in the sphere of culture, allowing the famous statement that domination has migrated into individuals.

In short, Pollock's thesis of organized capitalism takes on a tone in Adorno, to use the jargon, somewhat more pessimistic, insofar as such capitalism is the reflection of a fully managed world. The intervention of the state as an economic regulator and the role of science as an appendix of capital will find in the so-called mass culture the way in which capitalism extends its former domination, reaching now, more than before, the very soul of the worker. This worker, for the first generation of Frankfurtians, is still understood from the classical model of the theory of value. The proletarian whose subjectivity has been managed is the Fordist worker, encouraged to consume either refrigerators or Hollywood films. The notion of labor that underlies the critique of Adorno, Horkheimer and Marcuse is that of surplus-value-producing, alienated and modern labor. In the specific case of Marcuse, we see that in some moments of his work the transformations of categories that will later be imposed by immaterial labor are already visible, when he, in his interpretation of the *Grundrisse,* will

---

[102] About late capitalism for Adorno see, for example: Theodor W. Adorno, "Capitalismo Tardio ou Sociedade Industrial?" In *Sociologia*, editado por Gabriel Cohn (São Paulo: Ática, 1986a.), 62-75.

show himself as one of the pioneers of the critique of labor time as the core producer of capitalist wealth.[103]

In the second half of the 1960s, Habermas began to outline his version of late capitalism that would culminate in the work *Legitimationsproblem im Spätkapitalismus* which will be published in 1973.[104] But already in the work *Técnica e Ciência Enquanto Ideologia* of 1968 Habermas outlines not only his two-dimensional conception of society, guided by the distinction between labor and interaction, but also his critique of advanced capitalism.[105] Here, the Habermasian critique of some of the central concepts of traditional Marxism is already shown, as well as the incorporation of categories from functionalism that will run through all his future work, as is the case of the distinction between social integration and systemic integration.[106] A distinction that will also be important for your looking at late capitalism. Some changes in approach are manifested in relation to the first generation of Critical Theory:

> The Habermasian "variant" presents, on the contrary, a more complex physiognomy. Habermas proposes, in fact, to analyze the change in the form of the state in organized capitalism, contextually to a reconstruction of the new morphology of the crisis. Within this, it seeks to identify the specific role that the political system plays and the modality with which it competes to determine a dimension of the social conflict and the functioning of the economic mechanisms themselves, different from those manifested in the free-trade-competitive phase.[107]

In *Técnica e Ciência Enquanto Ideologia* Habermas expresses the understanding that it is possible to establish clear distinctions between liberal capitalism, the object of critique of Marxian political economy, and post-liberal or late capitalism, which will demand from Critical Theory new conceptual instruments of analysis. For Habermas, liberal capitalism found the legitimation of domination through the economic subsystem itself, in the sphere of the market, where free exchanges and wage labor were established. According to Habermas, this is the moment of capitalism in which "bottom-up" legitimation takes place. For him, Marx recognized the

---

[103] See: Herbert Marcuse, *A Ideologia da Sociedade Industrial* (Rio de Janeiro: Zahar, 1978).

[104] Jürgen Habermas, *Legitimation Crisis* (Cambridge: Polity Press, 1988).

[105] Habermas, *Técnica*.

[106] To see the distinction between different types of integration see: Jürgen Habermas, *Teoría de La Acción Comunicativa*, Tomo I (Taurus: Madrid, 1987a).

[107] Giacomo Marramao, *O Político e as Transformações* (Belo Horizonte: Oficina de Livros: 1990), 41.

institutional framework of society constituted from the relations of exchange of equivalents. In this way, the critique of political economy was at the same time an ideological critique that demystified the appearance of freedom in the capitalist exchange society. For him, since the end of the 19th century, two trends of development have occurred in the most advanced capitalist countries: the first is an increase in the interventionist activity of the state, which must guarantee the stability of the system, and secondly, a growing interdependence between research and technique, which transformed science into the main productive force:

> The expression "capitalism organized or regulated by the state" refers to two kinds of phenomenon, both of which can be attributed to the advanced stage of the accumulation process. It refers, on the one hand, to the process of economic concentration – the emergence of national and then multinational corporations and to the organization of markets for goods, capital, and labor. On the other hand, it refers to the fact that the state intervenes in the market when as functional gaps develop.[108]

This Habermasian conception of overcoming the liberal ideology phase of capitalism does not differ from what had already been diagnosed by the first generation of Frankfurtians. The realization that the state starts to fulfill a regulatory role in the market is something already present in Pollock. However, late capitalism for Adorno was identical to what he called an administered society, largely dominated by instrumental rationality. And this conception is not shared by Habermas. The overcoming of the liberal phase of capitalism does not mean the exhaustion of cultural modernity, on the contrary, the distinctions between the economic, political, and cultural spheres allow Habermas to understand late capitalism with nuances well differentiated from those of the first generation. In short: both Habermas, Pollock and Adorno agree on a new stage of capitalism that begins with the transformations of the beginning of the 20th century, notably about the new role of the state and the development of the productive forces. But the consequences of this finding will be different. The distinctive feature most clearly identifiable between the conceptions of late capitalism of the first generation of Frankfurtians and that of Habermas is precisely in terms of the conception of the forms of rationality present in contemporary society, since the Habermasian postulation of a communicative action as something effectively present in institutions of modernity inevitably leads him to another interpretation.

---

[108] Habermas, *Legitimation Crisis*, 33.

Another peculiarity of the Habermasian conception concerns the concept of crisis. For traditional Marxism, the economic crises resulting from the process of capital accumulation found an explanation within the economic sphere itself. Between the 1920s and 1930s, the debate within Marxism was intense regarding the concept of crisis, and it was precisely in the context of this debate that the different conceptions of Grossman and Pollock regarding the regime of capitalist accumulation at that historical moment began. Conceptions about the possible collapse of capitalism strongly marked the economic debate at the end of the 1930s, and Pollock's posture regarding a planned economy was constituted as a response to the mechanisms that the system found for its tendency to crisis.

Habermas, on the other hand, undertakes a new interpretation of the concept of crisis, at the same time as he seeks to visualize the trends associated with it in contemporary society. The historical context that supports the Habermasian reflection is different. The historical impact that most influences his conception of late capitalism is not the authoritarian state, but the Welfare State and post-war Keynesianism. Although it also analyzes state intervention in the market, the scope of its analysis is broader, as it includes a series of other historical factors, such as conscious attempts to pacify social conflicts.

We must first consider that the Habermasian theoretical approach no longer deals only with the old Marxian categories of the critique of political economy, but mainly considers the socio-analytical apparatus of Parsons' functionalism. The notion of system no longer refers exclusively to the economic system; although it remains subject to economic crises, these no longer correspond to systemic crises as understood by Marx and much of the Marxian tradition. For Habermas, while in liberal capitalism social integration is at risk because of an endemic crisis of the economic system, with late capitalism the role of the state as a controller of the crisis allows the emergence of new problems regarding its legitimacy. To the extent that with late capitalism the state began to replace those functions that were previously situated in the market itself, this now also began to fulfill the functions of systemic integration, through the middle power, but putting itself, therefore, also subject to trends of crisis.

The crisis tendencies pointed out by Habermas, when they are also expressed as crises of rationality and motivation, refer to the impossibility, on the part of the state, of fulfilling the expectations that it had created. Late capitalism thus begins to experience crises that no longer necessarily refer to the understanding that it was destined to collapse. And in this case, we can also try to understand in what sense a Critical Theory in the sense of Habermas faces the antagonisms present in contemporary society. Habermas pays attention to the fact that the social conflicts that will emerge with late capitalism no longer refer to those class conflicts situated in the economic system. To the extent that the state began to intervene as a pacifier of conflicts, it could not prevent the emergence of a new form of protest potentiality in the sociocultural system, the basis for the triggering of new social movements.[109]

There are two issues that we must highlight regarding the Frankfurtian trajectory. In the first place, both in the first generation and in Habermas, it seems to us that there was, in fact, no theoretical effort to understand the changes in labor category in the 20th century. In the case of Habermas, we understand that his central postulation, the one that sees labor in capitalism referring only to instrumental actions, also meant an abandonment of the attempt to understand labor historically and analytically in the constitution of capitalism. On the other hand, the non-explicit approach to the labor category is also present in Adorno and Horkheimer, largely as a result of their resistance to formal sociological analysis. At the same time, Adorno's emphasis on the role of culture in the accumulation regime of late capitalism takes on another approach in the Habermasian view. The critique of culture in the sense of critique of a sphere that produces cultural goods is replaced by an apprehension of the sociocultural system in which culture as commodity is not directly analyzed.

Unlike the conceptions seen above, Fredric Jameson will propose a new conceptualization for the expression late capitalism. In his work *Pós-Modernismo: a lógica cultural do capitalismo tardio*, published in the early 1990s, Jameson not only consolidates one of the most vehement analyses ever undertaken on the so-called postmodernity, but also articulates the analysis of contemporary culture with a new formulation for the notion of late capitalism.

Jameson's reflections, from this work, seek to refer to the changes that he understands to be taking place in contemporary culture, concomitant with changes in the capitalist mode of production itself, whose characteristics only manifested effectively from the beginning of the 1980s. For Jameson, postmodernism, therefore, does not refer to a style, as this term has often been interpreted, but refers to a historical period that derives from a moment of rupture in the very structure of world capitalism. Postmodernism thus refers to a period in which formal changes occur in the sphere of culture as a dialectical correlate of what comes to be called late capitalism.[110]

---

[109] See: Jürgen Habermas, *Teoría de La Acción Comunicativa*, Tomo II (Taurus: Madrid, 1987b), 555.

[110] See: Jameson, *Pós-Modernismo*, 16.

This conception of Jameson also radically differentiates him from other postmodern theorists, inasmuch as postmodernity is for him a historical periodization, in which the notions of market and mode of production play a central role. Late capitalism, as Jameson understands it, also differentiates it from those who invoke poststructuralist critique as an argumentative theoretical impulse, as is the case even with Negri and the authors of *Multitudes*. Jameson reclaims a reading of capitalism from categories that both poststructuralism and Habermas' critical theory consider outdated, with emphasis on the category of totality. Late capitalism for Jameson refers to a process of economic transformation that is at the same time a cultural transformation that gives meaning to it. According to Jameson:

> What happens is that aesthetic production today has become integrated into commodity production generally: the frantic urgency producing fresh waves of ever more novel seeming-goods (from clothing to airplanes), at ever greater rates of turnover, now assigns an increasingly essential structural function and position to the aesthetic innovation and experimentation. Such economic necessities then find recognition in the varied kinds of institutional support available for the newer art, form foundations and grants museums and other forms of patronage.[111]

Late capitalism does not mean, therefore, a phenomenon that begins at the end of the 19th century, as Habermas understands it, nor Adorno's administered society, but is defined as something much more recent, equivalent to the emergence of postmodernity. His conception of capitalism is largely based on Ernest Mandel's book.[112] Mandel identifies different phases of capitalism through a concept of "long waves" (or *Kondratiev waves*). There would be three distinct phases of capitalism: market capitalism (1847-1890), monopoly capitalism or imperialism (1890-1945), and the current moment (beginning from 1945 to the present), which many came to call capitalism post-industrial or multinational. Within these long waves of approximately fifty years, Mandel identifies periods of recession and slowing of growth, which we can include that started with the oil crisis of 1973.

Concomitant to this periodization, which refers to *the development phases of the capital,* Mandel also presents a periodization corresponding to the stages of technological development. Regarding this last form of periodization, Mandel asserts that we would be living today in a fourth

---

[111] Ibid., 30.
[112] Mandel, *O Capitalismo Tardio.*

moment of revolution, which related to the advent of microelectronics.[113] Jameson appropriates this periodization to claim that postmodernity is the equivalent of the multinational phase of capitalism, identifying with it the advent of postmodernity. We must consider that in Mandel's periodization, the so-called late capitalism began in the immediate post-World War II, a period that according to him was marked by a cycle of growth and expansion, as well as a phase of stability and overaccumulation.

This phase would have entered its stage of decline, something usual within long waves, between the end of the 1960s and the beginning of the 1970s. We must remember that most post-industrial society theorists point precisely to 1973 as a landmark in the transformation of the capitalist economy, an idea that we also share. Faced with this, it is not noticeably clear in what Jameson calls late capitalism the exact dimension of its periodization, if we consider, for example, that authors such as Harvey and Soja who see the passage to postmodernity precisely as something that only occurs between the 1970s and 1980s. Although they do not agree with Mandel's thesis about long waves, and do not keep the use of the concept of late capitalism, these authors refer to the historical moment that began in the1970s as an economic precondition for what they call postmodernism.

In any case, Jameson's book addresses precisely the cultural dominant of late capitalism, although it does not present us with an effectively convincing theoretical exposition of his concept of capitalism. Like the Frankfurtians, who are Jameson's main theoretical reference,[114] there is no explicit reference in all his work as to what kind of role the labor category starts to fulfill in this stage of capitalism's development. Although he mentions the need to keep class analysis alive, and recovers central concepts of Marxian dialectics, Jameson is not explicit about the way in which wealth and value are constituted in this new stage of capitalism.

In undertaking a rupture between modernity and postmodernity, the latter corresponding to a historical-economic periodization of the capitalist mode of production, Jameson not only seeks to restore the need for historicity to understand society, but also deals with categories that should be taken in terms of their abstraction character, that is, totality and mode of

---

[113] It is worth remembering that Mandel's study was originally published in Germany in 1972, in a historical phase prior to what we call here post-industrial society.

[114] This is, at least, our point of view, even though Jameson was influenced by post-structuralism, hermeneutics, Sartre, Althusser and others, our understanding is that his thinking is fundamentally inspired by the work of Theodor Adorno. See: Camargo, *Modernidade e Dominação*, 109-134.

production.[115] Totality and mode of production are thought as critical categories that enable the apprehension of the universal in the particular, such as the Marxian conception of exchange relations. It is in this way that postmodernity can only be understood through essentially modern categories, since the core of the processes of social domination, capitalist economic relations has remained unchanged in its historical content.

In more recent writings Jameson adds to his analysis of late capitalism concepts that were not clear before.[116] The first of these is globalization. The author in recent years has emphasized this concept as an equivalent to what he called in earlier works late capitalism, that is, the removal of all spatial and cultural barriers to the new stage of the accumulation process:

> What had happened then to highlight its relevance is that finally postmodernity and globalization are the same thing. These are two sides of the same phenomenon. Globalization embraces it in terms of information, in commercial and economic terms. And postmodernity, for its part, is the cultural manifestation of this situation.[117]

Jameson has also emphasized the process of financialization of capital pointing to Giovanni Arrighi's theses on financial capital and the differentiated role it occupies in the present stage of capitalism.[118] A third aspect that stands out in Jameson's thought is that of utopia. Although the theme is present throughout Jameson's intellectual journey, it seems that the author has given it increasing prominence.[119] On the one hand, Jameson is not very proactive in the political sphere, different from authors such as Habermas and Gorz, but on the other hand, he leads us to reflect on other dimensions of utopian thinking, such as that which emerges from contemporary literature. We will return in the sixth chapter, below, to the importance of Jameson for the analysis of what we call cultural production.

---

[115] See, for example: Fredric Jameson, *O Marxismo Tardio. Adorno ou a persistência da dialética* (São Paulo: UNESP, 1996).

[116] About this topic, see, for example: Fredric Jameson, *The Cultural Turn – Selected Writings on the Postmodern: 1983-1998* (New York: Verso, 2001b).

[117] Fredric Jameson, "Posmodernidad y globalización", Entrevista para *Archipiélago;* no. 63/2004. http://bibliweb.sintominio.net/pensamiento.jameson

[118] In the late 1990s Jameson came to associate his notion of late capitalism with the term's globalization and finance capitalism. In the essay "Culture and financial capital," Jameson associates the financialization of capital with the dematerialization of the world itself. See Jameson, *The Cultural Turn*, 143-172.

[119] Fredric Jameson, *Archaeologies of the Future* (London: Verso, 2005).

If we stick to the properly economic analyzes of capitalism, we should focus much more on thinkers like Claus Offe[120] and Robert Kurz.[121] And if we were to think about the explicit attempts to continue the model of Critical Theory, we will inevitably have to stick to the current work of Axel Honneth. However, the question that permeates the first part of this chapter is how we can understand the current phase of capitalism without losing sight of the theoretical instruments bequeathed by Critical Theory. In this sense, it is possible to say, preliminarily, that at least three fundamental aspects of the first Critical Theory still seem to us today to be significant for understanding late capitalism in its current phase.[122]

In the first place, it seems to us that none of the theories that followed the Frankfurtian critique of instrumental reason effectively proves its theoretical and historical limitation. On the contrary, what Adorno and Horkheimer called instrumental reason seems today to assume proportions that not even the authors themselves imagined. The evidence of instrumental rationality in contemporary society becomes something banal and naturalized within the scope of contemporary theory itself, since this rationality already exists in an inevitable way, there would be no reason to continue insisting on its critique. At the same time, we must continue to analyze, as we propose here, the extent to which contemporary capitalism gives us evidence of the existence of other forms of rationality.

Another aspect pointed out by Frankfurtians is the interference of politics and the state in the economic sphere. Although the so-called neoliberal capitalism uses the rhetoric of the market as the only possible reality for our historical existence, the current stage of capitalism shows us a state and political sphere entirely committed to the stabilization of the rules imposed by the market itself, that is, the end of the *Welfare State* does not mean that the state has abandoned the market. Differently from that, the articulation between economy and state occurs in the form of privatization of the latter and its regulation by the form of rationality that has always characterized the market in its liberal purpose.

---

[120] Claus Offe, *Capitalismo Desorganizado* (São Paulo: Brasiliense, 1995).

[121] Robert Kurz, *O Colapso da Modernização* (São Paulo: Paz e Terra, 1999).

[122] In our understanding, there are central aspects of the first Critical Theory, such as immanent critique and the *telos* of normativity that guide the reflection on the problems proposed here, in addition to the Adornian concepts of totality and not identity, as we will emphasize in the last chapter. As for the concept of late capitalism, we are saying that there are aspects of its first formulation that can still be useful for understanding the present, however, the main interest of our research is precisely to point to the need for a redefinition of this concept based on the new historical elements placed today.

The third and perhaps most relevant issue concerns the fact that the first formulations about late capitalism were at the same time the formation of a theory of domination, in which Marxian class domination was replaced by another, fundamentally situated in human subjectivity itself; bourgeois domination being above all the elimination of the autonomous subject from the historical objectivity constituted by the world of the commodity.

Also in this regard, we need to reflect on the relevance of the theses of the first generation of Critical Theory. The transformations of capitalism that we began to sketch in the first chapter show precisely that the analyses of the first Critical Theory took as their substrate an economic reality that no longer exists: that of industrial and monopoly capitalism. And a new issue emerged: immaterial labor as tending to be the main source of capitalist wealth. The validity of both the Frankfurtian epistemological instruments and the critique of capitalist domination they undertake will depend on thinking about how this theoretical apparatus survives in the face of an apparent exhaustion of the Marxian theory of value.

With regard to the relationship between late capitalism and historical periodization, the understanding postulated by Jameson is the closest to what we can understand today by that concept, that is, the historical phase marked in the early 1970s. On the other hand, its periodization, based on Mandel, brings some inaccuracies as to its interpretation. What Mandel refers to as a fourth historical phase of *technological development in capitalism,* Jameson names as a phase of *capital development.* Thus, late capitalism as he understands it corresponds to that fourth phase, and not to a phase of capital development.

David Harvey's definitions of postmodernity can be seen, as a historical periodization, as close to what we call late capitalism here in this work. Although this author refers to this phase only as a new stage in the process of capital accumulation, we propose as a theoretical hypothesis that the current historical mutation refers to the capitalist mode of production itself, where immaterial labor plays a significant role. The immaterial labor category is also not present in this author, but his descriptions of postmodern culture converge, to some extent, to our next argumentative steps.

CHAPTER 4

THE CONCEPT OF COGNITIVE CAPITALISM

The authors that approach immaterial labor, mainly in France, over the last fifteen years, have produced a vast bibliography on what they call cognitive capitalism. Aside from Gorz, Negri and Lazzarato, which we emphasized in the first chapter, we can mention Moulier-Boutang, Vercellone, Corsani, and others. Most of them were contributors to the magazine *Multitudes*, and many collaborated with the magazine *Futur Antérieur*. In Brazil, Giuseppe Cocco is explicitly associated.[123] The mutual understanding of this group of authors and the research programs they develop is that capitalism is currently experiencing a period of transition, which translates into the configuration of a new regime of accumulation and a change in the mode of production itself.

Regarding this last notion, these authors are similar in many ways to the arguments we have just seen regarding Jameson's concept of late capitalism, that is, that the ongoing transformations continue to revolve around the classical category of mode of production. Such similarities, which are also manifested in other aspects, find their limit when we remember that Jameson's late capitalism acquires its main meaning for its inseparability from the cultural turn, while for the authors of *Multitudes*, in general, what characterizes the new phase of capitalism is its biopolitical dimension, that is, it is about changes that concern the dimension of human life as a whole based on two central categories: that of immaterial labor and the *general intellect*.

We will then see some of the peculiarities pointed out by these authors, which are based on the ideas outlined so far regarding immaterial labor. However, in a quick mapping of contemporary production regarding the central themes discussed here, we perceive a variety of authors that to a significant extent converge to the diagnoses underway in this first decade of the 21st century. These are authors far from the Marxian tradition and whose theoretical production has a strong impact on the sociological debate and even on the media. It is enough to mention the work of Castells, and authors

---

[123] Giuseppe Cocco, *Trabalho e Cidadania* (São Paulo: Cortez, 2000).

not so present in sociological literature, but popular even outside the academic environment, such as Pierre Lévy[124] and Jeremy Rifkin. Although the exposition procedures of these authors do not have a greater sociological rigor, their studies provide significant elements to support the thesis regarding the exhaustion of industrial society.

In this sense, it is important to take up the arguments of an author mentioned in the first chapter, the North American sociologist Daniel Bell. Influential on the first theorists of postmodernism, Bell already pointed, more than thirty years ago, to the centrality of knowledge as the dividing mark for a new capitalism, or, as he prefers to say, for the advent of post-industrial society. The cognitive capitalism thesis bears a great deal of similarity to Bell's notion of post-industrial society. The success of Bell's work is largely due to his work being one of the first to talk about the exhaustion of the so-called paradigm of labor as something equivalent to the exhaustion of industrial society. Such exhaustion was at the same time a strong critique of Marxism, insofar as, in Bell's view, labor and class theories of value were no longer applicable in the new society.

According to the author himself, some critics of his work mistakenly understood that the core of his argument in this work was the transition from a society that produced goods to a society of services. This is what it might actually seem to any reader, inasmuch as Bell uses a large part of the book *The Coming of Post-Industrial Society* to show changes that took place mainly in the North American economy in the post-Second World War period regarding the displacement of labor activities from a sphere previously located centrally in factories to a growing sphere of services. However, we will see that for the author the core of his work is the postulation of knowledge as the new main aspect of contemporary society, with the growth of services being a characteristic that accompanies this change. According to Bell:

> A post-industrial society is based on services. Hence, it is a game between persons. What counts is not raw muscle power, or energy, but information. The central person is the professional, for he is equipped, by his education and training, to provide the kinds of skill which are increasingly demanded in the post-industrial society.[125]

Bell uses the expression post-industrial society and not capitalism because, according to him, his intention is to make an analysis that privileges the changes that were taking place in the technological sphere, or in what

---

[124] Pierre Lévy, *A Inteligência Coletiva* (São Paulo: Loyola, 2007).
[125] Bell, *The Coming*, 127.

Marx would call productive forces, while the expression capitalism would refer to those phenomena more consistent with production relations:

> One can see this by relating the concept of post-industrial society to that of capitalism. Some critics have argued that post-industrial society will not "succeed" capitalism. But this sets up a false confrontation between two *different* conceptual schemata organized along two different axes. The post-industrial schema refers to the socio-technical dimension of a society, and capitalism to the socio-economic dimension.[126]

It is evident, from the outset, that this is an interpretation of history distinct from historical materialism and that does not incorporate the plausibility of the existence of modes of production as an interpretative model of historical evolution. Its analytical schematization proposes the existence of pre-industrial, industrial, and post-industrial typologies, each of them corresponding to a specific emphasis not only on the main sectors of human activity, but also on the production of wealth itself. The schematization proposed by the author is in many aspects influenced by Weberian sociology. Bell states, for example, that the notion of post-industrial society is an *ideal type*, a conceptualization with which one tries to understand a certain historical formation with regard to technological development. He resembles Weber, and in a certain sense also Habermas, when he proposes a clear disjunction between spheres of human existence, notably between culture, polity, and economy:

> Analytically, society can be divided into three parts: the social structure, the polity, and the culture. The social structure comprises the economy, technology, and the occupational system. The polity regulates the distribution of power and adjudicates the conflicting claims and demands of individuals and groups. The culture is the realm of expressive symbolism and meanings [...] In the past, these three areas were linked by a common value system (and in bourgeois society trough a common character structure). But in our times, there has been an increasing disjunction of the three [...][127]

From this point of view, Bell understands that the analysis of post-industrial society concerns mainly the changes that take place in the sphere of social structure, notably with regard to the articulation between changes that occur in the economic sphere, the issues of the occupational system, and the new relations between theory and empiricism, especially in the relationship between science and technology. As for these levels of characterization of the social structure, we can establish numerous points of

---

[126] Ibid., lxxxviii.
[127] Ibid., 12.

approximation and distance between Bell's ideas and the authors we dealt with earlier.

From the outset, it is necessary to remember that Bell's methodological orientation is extremely far from the dialectic and ideas of a Marxist author like Jameson. We have seen how Jameson understands the transformations of contemporary society through an emphatic defense of the notion of mode of production, which separates him from most authors who postulate information and knowledge as central elements of contemporaneity.[128] On the other hand, this differentiation between spheres of value maintains similarity with the conceptions of Gorz and Habermas about the distinct types of rationality that characterize modernity. With Habermas still, there will be a strong similarity in terms of placing science and technique as the key elements of a new historical moment.[129]

Although we can consider Bell as one of the first theorists of society to pose problems that are at the center of the current debates on capitalism, the historical period analyzed by him is not identical, for example, to those who understand the year 1973 as a starting point of a new stage of capitalism, because his analyses are based on North American society in the previous two decades. But, in the author's view, this does not invalidate his analysis, on the contrary, the course of the Western world proved what he indicated to be a trend. In the 1999 Foreword of his work, Bell makes a long analysis of the historical consolidation of his diagnoses, both in terms of the role of knowledge and the vertiginous growth of the service sector. Some sectors have become crucial in terms of this transition from industrial to post-industrial society:

> The major expansion of services in contemporary society is "human services," primarily health and education. And both are the chief means today of increasing productivity in a society: education by advancing the acquisition of skills, particularly literacy and numeracy; health by reducing illness and making individuals more fit for work.[130]

---

[128] It would be more correct to say that Jameson differs from all those who have a non-Marxist orientation. If we compare him with the theorists of *Multitudes,* even if there is no agreement on the question of the centrality of knowledge, the latter also start from the notion of mode of production in their critique of capitalism.

[129] The similarities, however, stop there. The Habermasian concept of late capitalism covers a much longer period, already beginning with the decline of liberal capitalism. Furthermore, the Habermasian differentiation, as well as that of Gorz, has the sense of rescuing the normative content of modernity, which we cannot say about Bell.

[130] Ibid., xiv

Despite this, he rejects the notion of a society of services, as well as those of information and consumption. But the similarity between his conception and that of Castells, for example, is significant, as information occupies a principal place in what he calls post-industrialism. For Bell, the true nature of the transformations taking place in contemporary society is the differentiated role that knowledge and information play today in the economic sphere. Knowledge has become a central aspect not only in terms of what characterizes the new professional occupations of post-industrial society, but also becomes a new source of value. Although separated by a true ideological abyss, Bell will arrive at the same conceptual point as André Gorz, that is, the proposition that labor-value has been replaced by knowledge-value. The curious thing is that Bell does not make direct reference in his major work to the concept of immaterial labor, but in characterizing a society founded on the centrality of knowledge, he describes the same historical processes pointed out by Gorz and the theorists of *Multitudes*. According to Bell:

> A post-industrial society rests on a knowledge theory of value. Knowledge is the source of invention and innovation. It creates value-added and increasing returns to scale and is often capital-saving in that the next substitution (…) uses less capital and produces a more than proportional gain in output. Knowledge is a collective good (in particular basic research), and one can raise the question of whether a "social rent" is due to the class scientists who create the knowledge.[131]

Both Bell and other authors who defend the centrality of knowledge in the new economy point out with relative clarity to the fact that information and knowledge already had a fundamental role in previous phases of capitalism, but the differential aspect is in the way in which the new information and communication technologies began to be used in production from the 1970s. The emphasis is placed on the fact that, mainly from the advent of information technology in production, the type of labor that sustains the production process is preferentially cognitive and intellectual. At this point, we could ask ourselves in what sense the theories of post-industrial society or of the network society, differ from that Habermasian conception of late capitalism. Didn't this, for Habermas, mean a replacement of living labor by science and technology as the main productive forces? And it is worth remembering that this phenomenon for Habermas dates back to the beginning of the 20th century? Do what

---

[131] Ibid., xvii

Habermas calls technique and science have a different status than what those call information and knowledge?

We understand that one of the nodal points of differentiation lies in the fact that advanced capitalism for Habermas still presupposed an industrial base of production, preceding to the changes that only become visible in the last three decades.[132] However, there is a more significant difference regarding the very way in which the notion of knowledge is understood. First, we must consider the differentiation made between knowledge and *savoir* undertaken by Gorz, which is not visible in an author like Bell. For the latter, knowledge is shown to be something strongly associated with what takes place in large universities and research centers, that is, the production of scientific knowledge that imposes profound transformations in the working mechanisms of the economic sphere. In the same way, Castells understands that the network society is a result of the applicability of information technologies in production, whose main component is the knowledge that is associated with this informational process. As Castells says in the prologue to his main work:

> This book studies the emergence of a new social structure, manifested in various forms, depending on the diversity of culture and institutions throughout the planet. This new social structure is associated with the emergence of a new mode of development, informationalism, historically shaped by the restructuring of the capitalist mode of production towards the end of the twentieth century. The theoretical perspective underlying this approach postulates that societies are organized around human processes structured by historically determined relations of *production, experience, and power*.[133]

As for these theories that externally reinforce the thesis of cognitive capitalism, the distinctions made by Gorz find resonance in authors such as Pierre Lévy and Jeremy Rifkin, who extrapolate the problem of knowledge by incorporating *savoir* as a distinctive element of advanced capitalism. While the Marxian-influenced authors permanently resort to the concept of *general intellect* to refer to a knowledge that expresses the very crisis of the

---

[132] For Bell, knowledge presents itself as a natural result of technological advances and is accompanied by what he calls the "end of ideology." The Habermasian approach, on the contrary, from the beginning sought to show how this advance manifest itself as a new form of legitimation of domination in which the advance of productive forces, and the use of knowledge, bring with them the permanence of capitalist production relations, seeking to move away, in this way, from the traditional elegy of technical advance traditionally postulated by positivism.

[133] Castells, *A Sociedade em Rede*, 51.

capitalist paradigm of private property, the above authors, to the same extent that they converge on the idea of the so-called network society, minutely described by Castells, are little concerned with the forms of social domination that accompany the new role of knowledge. The new configuration of modern societies is driven by the advent of computers, associated with publicity and the instantaneous exchange of information, enabling the emergence of a knowledge that is general, common to society, and which constitutes a collective intelligence. According to Pierre Lévy, collective intelligence:

> It is an intelligence distributed everywhere, incessantly valued, coordinated in real time, which results in an effective mobilization of competences (...) An intelligence distributed everywhere: such is our initial axiom. Nobody knows everything, everybody knows something, all knowledge is in humanity. There is no reservoir of transcendent knowledge and knowing is not beyond what people know.[134]

Jeremy Rifkin, on the other hand, understands that the transition from industrial capitalism to cultural capitalism is the great question of our time. Rifkin's emphasis is less on the dimension of technological advancement and technoscience than on the cultural sphere. This is what he calls the era of access, that is, a historical moment in which the question of ownership changes, but the centrality of the market remains. Exchanges, however, no longer refer to the purchase and sale, to the possession of material goods. What is now in question for the author is the intellectual capital that dictates the rules of this transition period. For him, lived experiences, cultural experiences, become *commodities,* or the main commodity of the new era:

> We are making a long-term shift from industrial production to cultural production ... global travel and tourism, theme parks and cities, entertainment centers, wellness, fashion and cuisine, professional sports and games, music, film, television and the virtual worlds of cyberspace and electronically mediated entertainment of all kinds are fast becoming the center of a new hypercapitalism that commercializes access to cultural experiences.[135]

Although he refers at various times to the thoughts of Bell and Castells, Rifkin understands that the property-based economy is different from the network economy, whose characteristics dispense with property ownership in its most traditional sense. The changes in space and time of the access era imply, for example, not only a process of miniaturization of goods, a

---

[134] Lévy, *A Inteligência Coletiva*, 29.
[135] Rifkin, *A Era do Acesso*, 6.

phenomenon already emphasized by Bell, but also the reduction and prediction of the low durability of products. The same products, especially electronics, are produced to last a short and determined time. Commerce for Rifkin loses its modern qualities, even its more recent expressions like *shopping malls* to give way to cyberspace commerce. The flow of sales over the internet grows enormously every year and now moves billions of dollars. A considerable portion of consumers around the world prefer the comfort of receiving a certain product at home than going to buy it in a store, although we know that the latter is unlikely to disappear. Rifkin refers to the weight loss of current products as one of the expressions of the dematerialization process of society, and the clearest example is computers themselves.

Another significant aspect pointed out by Rifkin is what he calls the real estate downturn; an increasing part of companies prefer to rent their establishments, tools, machines, and real estate than own them. The figure of *leasing* and *franchising* is gaining increasing ground, the process through which the entrepreneur does not have the physical condition to produce a good or service, but only licenses himself for its use. This is something quite visible both in the Global North and South. For the author, who expresses himself in a language sometimes like that of the "wizards" of self-help and entrepreneurship, the network economy is different from the market-centered economy. Access, therefore, differs from possession, and there would be an exhaustion of the idea of ownership. Access refers primarily to the possession of information and knowledge, that is, intellectual capital. The age of access is characterized by the fact that concepts, ideas, and imagination replace the relevance of possession.

Although it is quite suggestive regarding our historical time, Rifkin's argument regarding the main axis of his thesis, that is, the replacement of property by access, seems questionable. The dematerialization of society regarding the possession of material goods, according to our understanding, only displaces the nucleus of production of wealth, which in the form of access continues to be privately appropriated. On the other hand, the way in which this author shows as diverse cultural experiences completely lose their character of autonomy in relation to market rules is significant. Such experiences are no longer just the cultural goods that Benjamin and Adorno talked about, but the lived experiences that no longer escape the logic of capital. Several authors have shown that tourism, for example, has tended to be one of the main sources of transformation of culture into commodity.

Both authors critical of capitalism and those who seem satisfied with technical progress and neoliberalism, when they emphasize the dematerialization of wealth and the priority of knowledge, manifest an optimistic view of what they call collective intelligence. The center of such optimism undoubtedly refers to the role of the internet in the process of human sociability in this first decade of the 21st century. The basic assumption is that forms of *savoir* and knowledge become communicable and widely accessible through the network, knowledge produced by society as a whole and that would be like the Marxian *general intellect.*

The researchers associated with the journal *Multitudes* are those who have effectively developed the notion of cognitive capitalism. At the center of this conception is the thesis of immaterial labor and its centrality in a new stage of capitalism. But, in what aspects are the conceptions of these authors as Moulier-Boutang, Vercellone, Corsani, Lazzarato are different from authors such as Bell, Castells and Rifkin, who also attribute a prominence of knowledge in the new stage of capitalism?

First, these authors are not talking about a post-industrial society or a network society, but about a capitalist society. We understand that the starting point finds in the continuity of an already old discussion present in contemporary sociology regarding the appropriation of the old Marxian distinction between productive forces and production relations. Roughly speaking, we can say that, on the one hand, there are those who advocate a certain independence from the productive forces, notably from technology, attributing to this the main reason for the changes that took place principally in advanced capitalist countries throughout the 20th century and with greater emphasis in the last decades. On the other hand, there are those who see technological advancement as something inseparable from production relations, with greater or lesser emphasis on the role of social classes, but ultimately understanding that social relations in advanced capitalism remain capitalist relations.

The question would be simple if the definition of capitalism were still as clear as it was in modernity. Remember that in the first chapter we emphasized that for Marx capitalism concerns a mode of production and not a mode of distribution. For Marx, the mode of production referred not only to the form of property, but to the model of labor that emerged with industrial society, guided by a certain form of division of labor and in which socially produced wealth is ineluctably deriving from the production of value, that is, of human labor as the fundamental source of this wealth. For Marx, in this way, the capitalist mode of production is related to a certain form of sociability whose core is labor time.

This leads us to suppose that when we affirm that the capitalist mode of production continues to exist because there is still private property, it is an insufficient condition to emphasize the capitalist character of the present. As we have seen before, the existence of wage labor and the extraction of surplus-value would also be insufficient conditions for a strong definition of capitalism, insofar as the economy of the immaterial tends precisely to replace these forms of production and exploitation with another regime of accumulation. If we follow Jeremy Rifkin's argument, for example, it will seem that we are nearing the end of capitalism, as we are moving towards the end of the modern idea of property.

We share here the thesis developed by Yann Moulier-Boutang: that capitalism in its current form expresses a phase of transition to a new capitalism. In it there would also be enough elements to talk about the coexistence of different modes of production in the same historical configuration. This idea is not foreign to Marxian thought. This stage of capitalism, which Moulier-Boutang understands as a third moment in its history, is still in a period of conformation, but it already has a set of characteristics that allow us to call it cognitive capitalism:

> Current globalization corresponds to the emergence, after 1975, of a third type of capitalism. This capitalism no longer has much to do with industrial capitalism which, at its birth between 1750 and 1820, broke with mercantile and slave capitalism. We are not experiencing a socialist transition. The irony of history is that we are everywhere experiencing a transition to a new kind of ... capitalism![136]

For Moulier-Boutang and Vercellone, the periodization of capitalism must consider the historical succession of different dominant configurations of capital accumulation. Thus, these authors initially point to an intermediate concept between the different notions of "modes of production" and "modes of development," conceiving their periodization within the framework of "historical systems of accumulation." Such systems refer to the stages of *mercantile capitalism*, which began in the mid-sixteenth century and lasted until the end of the eighteenth century, succeeded by *industrial capitalism* (1750-1973) and which now gives way to *cognitive capitalism*. It is evident in this periodization that it clearly differs from that proposed by Mandel regarding the phases of capital development, although it converges with the thesis of the so-called postmodern theorists (Jameson, Harvey, Soja) regarding the 1970s as the beginning of a new historical stage of capitalism.

Unlike Gorz, who sees cognitive capitalism not only as an expression of the crisis of the system but places a strong emphasis on the utopian potential of a "knowledge communism" that is historically close, Moulier-Boutang emphatically reinforces it as a passage to a new type of capitalism. It is, according to this author, a new form of accumulation, a new mode of

---

[136] Moulier-Boutang, *Le Capitalisme*, 24.

production, but also a new form of exploitation in the history of capitalism. In such capitalism, the role played by financialization, the structural changes in the dimension of the division of labor, the new order (post-Fordist) productive models, the role of innovation, the problems related to property rights, and especially the role of knowledge in the production of wealth.[137] As a result, categories such as externalities and biopolitics acquire meaning. Externalities are those external effects, positive or negative, which, instead of exerting a marginal influence on the production process, come to play a central role in a form of production in which cooperation and collective intelligence, as phenomena that are constituted outside the labor time. The externalities move from a secondary to a vital role in the production of wealth.

Just as late capitalism or globalization for Jameson is expressed by the significant importance of financial capital, for Moulier-Boutang and Vercellone cognitive capitalism does not escape the set of existing critiques of neoliberalism and the financialization of capital as a distinctive aspect of previous stages. For these authors, however, financial capital and its meaning in the accumulation process is a result, or something inseparable, from the current production regime, that is, from a production of wealth that arises primarily from the centrality of knowledge, and financialization *is one* of the aspects of this cognitive capitalism:

> On the other hand, the new productive model that emerges after thirty years is characterized equally by the amount of immaterial labor and by collective intelligence as the first fact of production or real substance of wealth as well as its value. These two characteristics are linked to the difficulty of measuring wealth as we could see until then.[138]

It is possible to state that financial capital, from the perspective of cognitive capitalism theorists, is not just a parasitic expression of capital, being an expression of an abstract labor still associated with the industrial period, but it is not something that is independent in a certain way of production. Financialization would be linked to a form of wealth production that does not necessarily correspond to the production of value. Even so, it is a way of capital accumulation that is increasingly independent of production in a material sense, that is, the centrality of knowledge corresponds to forms of speculation that do not have the production of goods

---

[137]Although the authors of *Multitudes* use the expression "cognitive," there is agreement with Gorz's distinction and precision about *knowledge and savoir*, that is, in fact, what is at issue for these authors is fundamentally the diffuse *savoir* produced by society.

[138] Moulier-Boutang, *Le Capitalisme*, 48.

as their substrate, insofar as money capital is largely disconnected from earlier forms of productivity.

In this sense, the conceptual hypothesis of financial capitalism appears to be insufficient from the perspective of Moulier-Boutang and Vercellone, insofar as we cannot simply minimize what is effectively new in this current process of financialization, considering it as a historical recurrence from phases of capitalist accumulation to financial dominance. On the other hand, the antagonism capital/labor should not be underestimated as a constitutive part of this process of financialization, replacing it with the contrast between the universal logic of expansion of money capital in the face of possible limits imposed by the political power of states. According to Vercellone:

> Financialization thus translates capital's attempt to adapt to changes that affect the most essential foundations of economic efficiency and value over those on which industrial capitalism rested. The purpose of finance cannot be thought of without approaching the crisis of industrial modalities of surplus value extraction. It is not only the cause, but also the consequence of the crisis of the Fordist wage relationship and the growth of the immaterial and intellectual content of labor. [...] The transformations in the division of labor, the new role of so-called immaterial assets and the increase in the power of finance are interdependent aspects of the current restructuring processes that capitalism knows.[139]

Cognitive capitalism is fundamentally the formation of a new productive model based on immaterial labor, or as Vercellone prefers to say on cognitive labor. Immaterial labor is thus once again defined as the activity whose main content is effectively knowledge. Or, to return to Gorz's distinction, *savoir*. *Savoir* that is socially produced as a collective intelligence and that, in the view of some authors, such as Gorz and Negri, resists being privately appropriated, at the same time that it enables the emergence of new forms of exploitation.

The immaterial is not limited to the result of labor, as a material or immaterial good, but refers to the content of the labor activity that determines the main aspect of valuing the commodity. It is the cognitive, symbolic, and intellectual activities that primarily contribute to valorization. A Nike shoe, for example, can be priced up to ten times higher than its competitor's brand, not because of its material attributes, but because of its symbolic attributes, and the complex network of cognitive valorization that

---

[139] Carlo Vercellone, « Sens et enjeux de la transition vers le capitalisme cognitif : une mise en perspective historique », *Multitudes*, Octobre, 2004, https://www.multitudes.net/Sens-et-enjeux-de-la-transition/

involves it, from the innovation processes in design, advertising, information about the consumer market, the apprehension of diverse cultures, the apprehension of the diversified consumer, etc. Ultimately, the knowledge.

But, again, we can ask: in what way does this conception differ from that of Daniel Bell? Aside from ideological distinctions, knowledge is treated here, even with regard to new information and communication technologies, as something also produced by society and not just by the application of science in production. Information and technology do not have an independent and autonomous existence in relation to the set of social relations. For the theorists of *Multitudes,* authors such as Bell and Castells manifest a kind of technological optimism, a variable of positivism and its ode to progress, which relegates to oblivion the inherent contradictions of capitalism, as if the productive forces had a development independent of the relations of production.

Cognitive capitalism dispenses with a distinction between information and knowledge that does not seem to be clearly pointed out by those authors. In principle, there is nothing new in saying that knowledge is the main aspect of production, nor in seeing this knowledge as something appropriated by the market, even in industrial society. The difficulty lies precisely in the complex and contradictory character that manifests itself in a type of knowledge that goes beyond the mercantile dimension as a result of its own nature, that is, as socially produced knowledge. Computers and the internet are configured as a modeling aspect of a certain form of sociability in which human knowledge and activities can be shared as something common by society. According to Vercellone:

> It is to specify the meaning of the current mutation that the concept of "cognitive capitalism" (capitalism + cognitive) was forged by calling into question the historical dimension and the conflicting dialectic between the two terms: the term capitalism designates the permanence, in this change, of the fundamental invariants of the capitalist system; in particular the driving role of profit and the wage relation, or more precisely, the different forms of dependent labor, on which the extraction of surplus rests; the term cognitive, in terms of itself, highlights the new nature of labor, the origins of value and the forms of property on which capital accumulation is based and the contradictions it engenders.[140]

There is no doubt that computers and the internet represent in this first decade of the 21th century one of the most fundamental aspects of such capitalism, according to the approach of all authors who refer to it. It is a general understanding among such authors that *software* is the manifestation

---

[140] Ibid.

par excellence of a new type of labor, essentially immaterial. In the case of creating *open-source software,* the cooperative dimension of the *general intellect* manifests itself as exemplary. It is therefore necessary to insist on both epistemological and normative reflection on this concept of capitalism. As we have seen so far, it is a different concept from that of late capitalism (in its various variables) insofar as it proposes a specific approach to the modern problem of the relationship between objectivity and subjectivity, or structure and action.

The thesis of cognitive capitalism depends directly on a new way of conceiving subjectivity. For the defenders of this concept, the idea of biopower is central, as well as questions related to a new territoriality, the problems of copyright and the new outlines underway in the field of genetic research. In the following pages, we will try to establish a dialogue between the appropriation of subjectivity as carried out by the critical theory of society and the way it is understood by the main cognitive theorists. From this, we intend to show the subtle, but decisive difference between knowledge (and *savoir*) and culture, recovering our previous concept of late capitalism and the way in which it is compatible with the concept of immaterial labor.

CHAPTER 5

INTERMEZZO:
SUBJECTIVITY AND THE IMMATERIAL

Theorists of the immaterial postulate subjectivity and its production as a central aspect for the formation of cognitive capitalism. In the production of the immaterial, subjectivity has three forms of unfolding that we consider relevant: as a producer of wealth, as the epicenter of a late form of domination and exploitation, and as a possibility of utopia. We are talking of a new subjectivity in capitalism. As Lazzarato and Negri say:

> If today we define workers' labor as an abstract activity linked to subjectivity, it is nevertheless necessary to avoid any misunderstanding. This form of productive activity does not belong only to the most qualified workers: it is also about the use value of labor power, and more generally the form of activity of each productive subject in post-industrial society. We can say that in the skilled worker, the "communication model" is already determined, constituted, and that its potentialities are already defined; while in the young worker, in the precarious worker, in the unemployed youth, it is still a matter of pure virtuality, of a capacity that is still undetermined, but which already contains all the characteristics of post-industrial productive subjectivity.[141]

We know that enunciating the concept of subjectivity as a central aspect for understanding society is not only not new in the context of contemporary social theory, but also permeated with problematizations, whose theoretical complexity can easily lead us to inaccuracies. From Weber to recent theories about the new social movements,[142] the entire history of Marxism, the psychoanalysis, the post-structuralism, the phenomenology, and the Frankfurt

---

[141] Lazzarato and Negri, *Trabalho Imaterial*, 25-6.
[142] See, for example: Jeffrey Alexander, "Ação Coletiva, cultura e Sociedade civil: secularização, atualização, inversão, revisão e deslocamento do modelo clássico dos movimentos sociais." *Revista Brasileira de Ciências Sociais* 13, nº 37, (junho 1998): 5-32 and, François Dubet, *Sociologie de L'Expérience*, (Paris : Editions du Seuil, 1994).

School itself, just to remember some models, explored subjectivity as something central to understanding of society. As Adorno said when talking about the role of philosophy after the moment in which it did not take place,[143] possibly returning to the subject of subjectivity is to insist precisely in the face of a social objectivity that has only partially changed since the emergence of the modern capitalism.

The social-theoretical approach to subjectivity inevitably leads us to the philosophical discourse of modernity itself, exemplarily thematized by Habermas, as well as to the *Aufklärung* tradition, and to the way in which German idealism also emerges as one of the founding moments of Marxian thought. In the Marxian tradition, human subjectivity is interpreted firstly as a dimension of the production of consciousness, that is, as a dimension inseparable from material objectivity, notably, the objectivity that is historically manifested in the capitalist mode of production. As Marx and Engels say in their critique of Feuerbach:

> In direct contrast to German philosophy which descends from heaven to earth, here we ascend from earth to heaven. That is to say, we do not set out from what men say, imagine, conceive, nor from men as narrated, thought of, imagined, conceived, in order to arrive at men in the flesh. We set out from real, active men, and on the basis of their real life-process we demonstrate the development of the ideological reflexes and echoes of this life-process.[144]

It is also in the sphere of critique of subjectivity as an expression of the capitalist mode of production that the critique of commodity fetishism is manifested[145] as the concept of alienation had already gained prominence. It is these processes that acquire centrality, for example, Lukacs's reading of Marx in *História e Consciência de Classe*. The way in which subjectivity becomes centrally constitutive of the concept of reification is a central aspect of this work and of all Lukacsian thought in the 1920s. It is worth remembering that the entire debate that took place in that decade regarding the historical subject which involved thinkers such as Rosa Luxemburg, Karl Korsch, Ernst Bloch, and others, always had at its center the problem of subjectivity and the way in which German idealism was at the origin of the Marxian concept of *praxis.*

A significant part of Marxist literature in the 20th century, with emphasis on the Frankfurt School, sought to deal with this challenge of understanding the role of subjectivity in the very constitution of capitalist

---

[143] Theodor W. Adorno, *Dialéctica Negativa* (Madrid: Taurus, 1984), 11.
[144] Marx and Engels, *The German Ideology*, 47.
[145] See: Karl Marx, *O Capital I* (São Paulo: Nova Cultural, 1985a).

social relations. This challenge meant that the critique of Marx's political economy had to approach other dimensions of the critique, as in the case of the critique of rationality, which express the increase in complexity of capitalist relations from the beginning of the 20th century. In the scope of the Marxian tradition, or dialectics, the epistemological bases informed by materialism maintain the understanding of the subjectivity always dependent on the objectivity of society, which is not the case, for example, of those forms of thought such as post-structuralism.

This complexity involved both the attempts to bring Marxism closer to psychoanalysis[146] and the exacerbation of the concept of reification to that of instrumental rationality.[147] From the 1970s onwards, these forms of apprehension of human subjectivity that still support the Marxian model as the main reference will be the object of theoretical contestation through different paths, limiting us here to pointing out those that seem to us to be the most expressive for our argument. On the one hand, we have the maturation of the post-structuralist discourse, with emphasis on Derrida, Deleuze and Foucault, who each in their own way, tried to elucidate a notion of subjectivity that could no longer be understood through the notions of subject and object, or through the explanatory primacy of the economic process of production. At the same time, objections also arise to the Freudian model and psychoanalysis.[148] It is possible to say, in a somewhat laconic way, that subjectivity is the great philosophical theme of modernity.

In the debates and exchanges that exist between philosophy and sociology, Habermas played a fundamental role in contemporary social theory.[149] Habermas undertook the most elaborate critique of the notion of

---

[146] See, for example: Herbert Marcuse, *Eros e Civilização* (São Paulo: Círculo do Livro, 1982).

[147] Adorno and Horkheimer, *Dialética do Esclarecimento.*

[148] The philosophy of the 20th century was marked by numerous attempts to break with the modern molds of subjectivity as it had been treated since Kant, or even Descartes. The philosophy of language with Wittgenstein, phenomenology with Husserl, hermeneutics with Gadamer, are some of these attempts that influenced the countless attempts to abandon the so-called philosophy of the subject. But we cannot fail to mention the most impressive approach to the phenomenon of subjectivity in the 20th century that was Freud and psychoanalysis, later problematized by Jacques Lacan. About the critique of Freudian thought, see: Gilles Deleuze e Félix Guattari, *O Anti-Édipo: Capitalismo e Esquizofrenia* (Rio de Janeiro: Imago, 1976).

[149] We cannot forget that in the history of sociology the so-called subjectivity has already reached its maximum level of importance since its classical phase with Weber. The entire Weberian method and sociology have the notion of subjectivity as their central aspect. See: Max Weber, *Economia e Sociedade.* Vols. I e II (São Paulo: Ed. UNB, 2004).

subjectivity, which came from a tradition that passed through Hegel, Marx, Lukács and Adorno, to affirm intersubjectivity as the new explanatory nexus for the processes of sociability of late capitalism.[150] The abandonment of the philosophy of consciousness, the epistemological equivalent of the abandonment of the production paradigm, points to the incorporation of new epistemological point of view, originating mainly from the philosophy of language, in the problematization concerning the subject. The latter loses strength not only as a political category,[151] but also as an epistemological one, shifting the traditional problem of consciousness to that of the constitution of communicative action through linguistic intersubjectivity.

In the two-dimensional conception of society shared by Habermas and Gorz, the apprehension of human subjectivity is inseparable from their conceptions of distinct types of rationality. While the world of labor is an expression of instrumental or economic rationality, the lifeworld is for them the sphere of a potentially liberated subjectivity. For both Habermas and Gorz, at this stage of his thought, this subjectivity no longer refers to that transcendental subjectivity of German idealism, nor to the socially produced consciousness of Marxian discourse. Subjectivity is somehow fragmented, without reason losing its universal character, basically expressing itself in two forms of rational action: those induced by systemic or heteronomous imperatives, and those produced by intersubjectivity, or by the experience of the lifeworld, potentially autonomous.

The notion of intersubjectivity represents another epistemic model compared to that of the *Enlightenment* heritage, although it does not maintain the same meaning in the different authors discussed here. In Negri's case, for example, the communicative dimension of immaterial labor does not have the sense of abandoning the so-called productivist model but seeks to point to a new dimension of labor relations in which they become essentially intersubjective, maintaining labor, ambiguously, a central element in the production of capitalist wealth. Regarding the emphasis on the communicative aspects of human sociability, Negri, as we have emphasized before, does not see communication from a theory of action, nor is he explicit about the epistemological distinction between subjectivity and intersubjectivity.

---

[150] Habermas, *Teoría de La Acción Comunicativa I.*

[151] When we speak here of critique of the subject, we should not understand it as this expression became known in the context of structuralism and post-structuralism, ways of thinking very different from those proposed by Habermas. At the same time, critique of the subject from a structuralist perspective was already very present in the field of Marxism, during the 1960s, with Althusser and others.

Despite their differences, we have already seen that both Negri and Gorz attribute a fundamental role to subjectivity in their characterizations of immaterial labor. The thesis, which would already be present in the *Grundrisse*, that capitalist wealth is also based on free time, necessarily attributes to the sphere of subjectivity a key role in the new conditions of capitalist productivity, even when referring to the notions of mass intellectuality and overall productivity. One of the main exponents of the theory of cognitive capitalism will agree with him:

> But everything changes when work, becoming increasingly immaterial and cognitive, can no longer be reduced to a simple expenditure of energy carried out in a given time. In fact, in cognitive capitalism, the main source of value now resides in the creativity, versatility and inventiveness of employees and not in fixed capital and routine labor.[152]

Different, however, from those currents of thought that attribute a fundamental importance to the Marxian concepts of alienation and estrangement, the problems raised regarding immaterial labor mainly concern a subjectivity no longer directly linked to the dimension of human labor, or, to the material labor settled in economic rationality. If we think about activities such as marketing and advertising, which are core to the concept of immaterial, we see a double dimension of subjectivity: at one point it is the very productive base of wealth built on symbols and images, guided by an extreme economic rationality, while marketing and advertising enter the life space of individuals, in all their moments of non-labor and leisure. The subjectivity of the worker, for both Gorz and Negri, is on the other hand productive in a positive sense, that is, as something that goes beyond the classical way of conceiving wage labor. And for Lazzarato and Negri, this possibility was already present in the *Grundrisse:*

> It is on this basis that the question of subjectivity can be posed as Marx does, that is, as a question concerning the radical transformation of the subject in its relationship of simple subordination to capital. On the contrary, this relationship is posed in terms of independence in relation to the labor time imposed by capital. Secondly, this relationship is posed in terms of autonomy in relation to exploitation, that is, as a productive, individual, and collective capacity, which manifests itself as a capacity for enjoyment. The classic category of labor proves to be absolutely insufficient to account for the activity of immaterial labor.[153]

---

[152] Vercellone, "É na reversão".
[153] Lazzarato and Negri, *Trabalho Imaterial*, 30.

In Negri and Lazzarato's view, subjectivity is not just a source of productivity in the sense of something that is appropriated by capital. Subjectivity is also general social productivity, diffused throughout society as a whole. It is in this way that it has the possibility of becoming a *mass intelligentsia*, in a collective subjectivity that also has a utopian dimension and communist potential. But it is no longer about that active Marxian subjectivity that should express itself as the self-consciousness of a class, of a historical subject. In Negri, this diffuse subjectivity will seek, when brought to the sphere of politics, the concept of the *multitude* as something no longer related to class antagonisms and dialectical thinking, but an expression of forces of resistance and dissidence of the *Empire:*

> If labor tends to become immaterial, if its social hegemony is manifested in the constitution of the *General Intellect*, if this transformation is constitutive of independent and autonomous social subjects, the contradiction that opposes this new subjectivity to the capitalist domain (if at all way one wants to designate it in post-industrial society) will not be dialectical, but alternative (…) the antagonism presents itself in the form of a constituent power that reveals itself as an alternative to the existing forms of power.[154]

According to Gorz, in turn, the subjectivity of the immaterial is also present in the relationship between production and consumption. The formation of the consumer through activities such as advertising and marketing, represents in cognitive capitalism a more than considerable portion of capitalist investments. The production of wealth depends directly on a subjectivity that no longer refers to an apprehensible alienation in time and in the workspace, but a subjectivity that encompasses all life, making it the producer of wealth par excellence.[155] It is no longer a result of the world of labor, but on the contrary, it is labor that depends on a subjectivity forged in the lifeworld.

The difference between this conception and that of the Frankfurtians lies in the fact that advertising is no longer just a visibility mechanism for industrially produced material goods, being thus an extension of industrial production. It is now not only the producer of new consumption needs but is the very purpose of consumption for its own sake. Advertising, images,

---

[154] Ibid., 36.
[155] The concept of reification in Lukács already pointed to the fact that the alienation of labor does not refer only to the direct experience of labor. Reification, as he understood it at that historical moment, did not have the character of a "productive" phenomenon, but was part of the mechanisms of reproduction of capital that continued to have, however, the material production of commodities as its analytical and structural core.

the cultural apparatus that permeates the entire non-labor daily life, becomes the main basis for the production of capitalist wealth. Subjectivity can no longer be apprehended as a result of the material metabolism between man and nature, it is the very basis of productivity.

The problematization posed mainly by Negri, Gorz and the theorists of *Multitudes* concerns the fact that the very concept of immaterial brings as its founding element the dimensions of communication, cooperation, creativity, and the use of the intellect as its central aspects. Knowledge, in the sense pointed out by them, can also be understood as an expression of human intersubjectivity, although this concept rarely appears in their exposition. For Lazzarato and Negri, subjectivity assumed the figure of a mass intellectuality, constituted in the set of social relations, being itself the source of productivity.

But Negri, Hardt and Lazzarato no longer refer to subjectivity in the traditional sense allied to the philosophy of consciousness. It would also be, in the case of these authors, as well as in Habermas and Gorz, much more appropriate to speak of intersubjectivity. The emphasis of its understanding is the processes of cooperation and communication that characterize the new productivity, therefore, the way in which individuals share knowledge and information in an intersubjective network, always mediated by language, which also comes to define immaterial labor:

> In other words, it can be said that when labor is transformed into immaterial labor and immaterial labor is recognized as the fundamental basis of production, this process does not invest only in production, but in the entire form of the "reproduction-consumption" cycle: the immaterial labor is not reproduced (and does not reproduce society) in the form of exploitation, but in the form of reproduction of subjectivity.[156]

But this subjective sharing emphasized by the theorists of *Multitudes* is quite different, it is worth insisting, also from intersubjectivity and the Habermasian *Lebenswelt*. It is not a sphere in which spontaneous interactions free from domination take place, but rather lived experiences that are themselves productive, bringing as a consequence the need to think about another power that would be hegemonic today, the biopower. Biopower appropriates human life as a whole, making it, itself, a source of productivity. We are speaking, therefore, of a conception of subjectivity much more indebted to Deleuze and Foucault.[157] For Hardt and Negri, the Habermasian distinction between system and lifeworld is not appropriate, as globalization

---

[156] Lazzarato and Negri, *Trabalho Imaterial*, 30.
[157] See, especially: Michel Foucault, *Naissance de la biopolitique* (Paris: Col Hautes Etudes: Seuil/Gallimard, 2004).

would have undermined this differentiated point from which to think about emancipation, giving way to a resistance sought in the *multitude itself.* This distance from Habermasian thought is at the same time an insistent refusal of dialectics:

> For the real clarification of this scene, we are most indebted to a series of French philosophers who reread Nietzsche decades later, in the 60s [...] Not the dialectics, but refusal, resistance, violence and the positive affirmation of being now marked the relationship between the location of the crisis in reality and the adequate response.[158]

Unlike Habermas and Gorz, who identify labor in capitalism in the sphere of heteronomy, Negri and his companions do not share the position regarding the exhaustion of labor as the main source of productivity, that is, the overcoming of the value theory proclaimed by them does not mean the abandonment of labor as an ontological category and central to the understanding of contemporary society.[159] For Negri, the subjectivity that is associated with current forms of labor continues to support the modern ideal of an emancipatory potential:

> Conversely, rather than commence from the standpoint of a historically sedimented dialectic, in which subjectivity is progressively domesticated (toward the very limit of its own disintegration) by the administrated society's "culture industry," Negri's variation of autonomist Marxism maintains that contradictions within the workplace have progressively given rise the development of an oppositional working-class subjectivity.[160]

When approaching the concept of cognitive capitalism, we see that Negri and Gorz, through slightly different strategies, defend the idea that the immaterial brings with it a kind of communism of *savoir*, precisely because *savoir*, when it becomes the main productive force, is something that can hardly be privately appropriated. *Savoir* is not constituted for them as an immediate producer of surplus value, but on the contrary, when it becomes general productivity, a manifestation of the social individual, the subjective chain of this *savoir*, which we can call "brain cooperation," becomes also emancipatory potential. At the same time, Hardt and Negri's

---

[158] Hardt and Negri, *Empire*, 378.

[159] It would be foolhardy, therefore, to conceive the theses on immaterial labor as a mere result of the debates regarding the end of the production paradigm. Despite similarities with the general idea regarding the "end of labor," Hardt and Negri strive to show just the opposite of this idea.

[160] David Sherman, "The Ontological Need: positing subjectivity and resistance in Hardt and Negri's Empire." *Telos*, 128, (Summer 2004): 145.

conception of the multitude as the *locus* of a constituent power – that is, the
conception that, in the face of the new type of sovereignty that is expressed
in the imaginary, the political force of the multitude is opposed – does not
express with clarity, in our understanding, in which collective-historical
subjects manifest this resistance force of which they repeatedly speak. It is
true that, according to them, this force of resistance is always associated
with the concept of subjectivity, but in the specific case of Negri, this is
often highlighted in terms of its aspects of resistance, resulting in a few
moments of a self-critique of this subjectivity regarding the cultural aspects,
which should also be analyzed.

On the other hand, also taking into account this normative dimension of
the authors discussed here, we must be emphatic about the fact that this
subjectivity that Negri and Lazzarato call productive is also an objection to
the Habermasian theory of communicative action. According to Giuseppe
Cocco:

> It is not political action that integrates the model of labor, as announced by
> H. Arendt, nor the communicative action of the Lifeworld that is colonized
> by instrumental rationality, as announced by Habermas; it is labor that
> becomes action as the ability to adapt to the unpredictability of starting
> something anew and producing linguistic performances. In its integration with
> political action, communicative action absorbs instrumental reasoning.[161]

The hypothesis that we will develop in the following chapters is that
what thinkers of the immaterial call subjectivity refers mainly to
experiences that occur in the cultural sphere. When we speak of immaterial
labor in the sense of cooperation, information, creativity, etc., we refer to
properly cultural social experiences. Such experiences, which permeate the
very idea of subjectivity, would be different from those that characterize the
economic sphere, as Gorz and Habermas think. When referring to the
subjectivity associated with immaterial labor, we would no longer be
talking, it is worth insisting, of the alienated subjectivity of the modern
worker, or even of reification in the way Lukács and Adorno thoughts. That
does not mean their abandonment, but the need to think about reification
within the framework of a different historical context today.[162]

We defend the idea that the labor category, which supported the
reflection of the different thinkers of late capitalism that we analyzed in
Chapter 3 have been changing radically in the current historical configuration.

---

[161] Cocco, *Trabalho e Cidadania*, 123.
[162] As has been the effort, for example, of Axel Honneth in one of his most recent
labors. See Honneth, *Luta por Reconhecimento*. After this labor there were
significant changes in Honneth's thinking, which we will not develop here.

Immaterial labor, in its historical context, does not only refer to instrumental actions limited to the space and time typical of industrial production, but to the set of social experiences that demarcate human life in a broad sense.[163] Hence Negri's insistence on the concept of biopolitics. The worker's subjectivity must now be apprehended in terms of its own productive potential: subjectivity is a producer of wealth, although not necessarily a producer of value.

Mainly supported by Foucault, *Multitudes theorists* have interpreted this productive subjectivity as the passage from the disciplinary society to the control society. Foucault's studies on disciplinary power would refer to the stage of capitalism situated mainly in the 18th and 19th centuries, while in the post-Second World War capitalism, in its neoliberal form, would be formatting ways of subjectivation no longer explained by the existence of disciplinary institutions, but biopower becomes visible in the very mode of existence of the public space, in social network relationships, in communicational processes.[164] According to Deleuze:

> It is control societies that are replacing disciplinary societies. "Control" is the name that Burroughs proposes to designate the new monster, and that Foucault recognizes as our near future. Paul Virilio also constantly analyzes the ultra-rapid forms of control in the open, which replace the old disciplines that operated in the duration of a closed system.[165]

But if the lifetime, the time of not labor as well, has become all of it in productive potential, where can we find the possibility of an autonomous

---

[163] A statement that does not, therefore, refute the concept of reification of the first generation of critical theorists. The problematization regarding this concept is due to the fact that in our argument, free time, of non-labor, is not just a time of reproduction that has abstract labor as its necessary substrate.

[164] Foucault's view of the society of control and its relationship to neoliberalism gained new impetus with the publication in 2004 of *Naissance de la biopolitique,* a subsequent publication of a considerable part of Negri's texts, for example, that we are analyzing. In this work, Foucault presents more solid elements for us to think, based on *homo oeconomicus,* the notion of human capital, so central to the theory of the immaterial, and more than that, a differentiated view of the relationship between economics and politics in neoliberal era. Foucault defends the idea, in short, that the political has completely transformed itself into something ruled exclusively by the logic of the market, with no other rationality than that of the market. In this respect, Foucault's view is close to the idea that we defend here regarding the impossibility of distinguishing between the "value spheres of modernity", although Foucault's emphasis is on the "political" and we propose this indistinction regarding to the "cultural."

[165] Gilles Deleuze, *Conversações 1972-1990* (Rio de Janeiro: Ed. 34, 1992), 220.

subjectivity? The everyday experiences that form *savoir,* for Gorz, at a certain moment in his work, are what supports this possibility and it is in this sense that the phenomenological bias, especially that inspired by Sartre, will pose problems that are also relevant for us to think about the relationship between subjectivity and immaterial labor, insofar as the temporality of the lifeworld is for Gorz, first and foremost, a time of existential experiences, very different, it should be remembered, from the Habermasian conception of the *Lebenswelt.*

From what we have explained in the last pages, it seems to be easy to infer the conclusion that when we talk about productive subjectivity we are talking almost exclusively about a certain form of power or domination that is concomitant with the advent of the immaterial. But we have also seen, on the other hand, that any idea of emancipation, for the main theorists of the immaterial, moves from the analysis of the historical objectivity of the advance of productive forces to the apparently optimistic apprehension that such advance is concomitant with the emergence of a mass intellectuality whose meaning is given by the realization that we are currently experiencing a new subjectivity. When we try to follow the steps taken by such authors, we are faced with a certain epistemological approach established by them that distances us, in a certain sense, from other aspects of contemporary thought that could also be analyzed in the context of the immaterial, as for example, the destiny of the concept of ideology.

There are certain aspects of contemporary society, however, that cannot fail to be related to the processes of transformation of capitalism driven by the centrality of immaterial labor. Such questions, which also involve the subject of subjectivity, have been dealt with within the scope of the tradition of critical theory of society, notably with Habermas and Honneth. We refer here to the problems of identity, such as gender and race, which have been increasingly analyzed through categories that are built on the margins of the Marxian paradigm, and Habermas, in the 1980s, was one of the first to offer new conceptual bases for understanding the historical role of such problems. Likewise, as we shall see later, Honneth's theory of recognition is equally relevant to the whole of our argument.

The questions raised here about the "new subjectivity" can also be understood from other critical parameters, different from the model proposed by the theorists of cognitive capitalism. His approach will begin, however, with the attempt to understand the effectiveness, to remind us of Hegel, who is making it possible. Our task is to understand, even if in general terms, what these ongoing transformations in capitalism consist of, to try to show the adequacy of our hypothesis about the inseparability between immaterial labor and cultural production.

The emphasis that we give to the concept of subjectivity and that we share with authors who approach the theme of the immaterial, such as Gorz, Negri and Lazzarato, represents the challenge of understanding a historical moment in which the objectivity of the capitalist mode of production is changing in its most central foundations: the constitution of commodity, value, and wealth. The problem is that the objectivity of such categories is no longer expressed in the form of entities or material relationships, as is visible, for example, in an industrial production process. This does not mean to say that world hunger, forms of social exploitation and exclusion, secular forms of injustice and disrespect, are not real and objective phenomena. They are even more real than at any other time in history.

It seems to us, however, that what Marx evoked in some passages of the *Grundrisse,* regarding the possibility of the capitalist mode of production creating the conditions so that its most fundamental element, abstract labor, contradictorily ceases to be the basis of production of wealth, is something that must be investigated as equally real and effective, when we are faced with the inseparability of immaterial labor and contemporary culture.

CHAPTER 6

INDUSTRY AND POST-CULTURE INDUSTRY

We start from the hypothesis that the phase started in 1973 in the history of capitalism it is a new expression of late capitalism, which we will call here late transitional capitalism.[166] This is a new stage of capitalism, which is still in progress as far as its configuration is concerned, and we understand it to be a transition stage in the history of world capitalism, whose historical outcome is not possible to predict, but only to point out new aspects already consolidated and irreversible, notably in terms of the development of productive forces. After presenting the theses regarding cognitive capitalism, which in various aspects hold our reflection, we propose to recover the concept of late capitalism. We start from the understanding that what we call transition is at the same time the crisis of capitalism, in which the visibility of its financialization is just one of the characteristics presented today. The main characteristic of this phase, as we propose, is the emergence of cultural production as the epicenter of a new production of wealth.

The first difficulty we face concerns the very sense of culture with which we propose to deal. The meaning used here refers more specifically to the universe of cultural goods, or the dimension of art, that is, literature, painting, architecture, etc., to the detriment of a more anthropological meaning, although we are dealing with a difficulty that is proper to the term culture, as Williams[167] and Eagleton [168] put it. The other possible sense is that in which culture is understood as the set of values, beliefs, knowledge, and *savoirs*, that refer to our daily lives, to the universe of symbolic reproduction of society. Although this last meaning must also be taken into account, insofar as its separation is not always possible, we want to emphasize the way in which the economic sphere is confused with the

---

[166] From now on, when we talk about late capitalism, we refer to it, in this sense, as an attempt to reconceptualize it in the face of the new historical phase, and no longer based solely on the previous definitions that we try to attribute to the concept. We indicate such sense at the end of chapter 3.

[167] Raymond Williams, *Cultura* (São Paulo: Paz e Terra, 2000).

[168] Terry Eagleton, *The Idea of Culture* (Oxford: Blackwell Publishing, 2000).

aesthetic dimension, that is, how the aesthetic comes to encompass the set of sociability relations in capitalism, demonstrating that it no longer has any autonomy in relation to the economic and even political sphere. During his attempt to clarify the distinctions between civilization and culture, and the various meanings that the latter has taken in the course of historical development (such as the distinction between Culture and culture), Eagleton says:

> As the anthropologist Marshall Sahlins observes, in a smack at the Marxist base/superstructure model, "In the tribal cultures, economy, polity, ritual and ideology do not appear as distinct *systems*." In the postmodern world, culture and social life are once again closely allied, but now in the shape of the aesthetics of the commodities, the spectacularization of politics, the consumerism of life-style form, the centrality of the image, and the final integration of culture into commodity production in general.[169]

In this case, it is worth anticipating that the two-dimensionality between economy and culture, largely inherited from the Weberian distinction between the spheres of values of modernity, gives way to a dialectic of totality which consists in affirming that the capitalist mode of production, in its present stage, has eliminated the possibilities of such a distinction. This sense that we adopt, therefore, is also different from the one in which the emphasis is given to the idea of multiculturalism, or even the emphasis on culture as the core of *identity politics.* The emphasis on a concept of culture as something fundamentally related to identity is also present in both Habermas and Honneth. Pierre Bourdieu will have a different approach, understanding culture as *habitus,*[170] as patterns of behavior symbolically shared by members of a certain field, a definition that also interests us, insofar as it also refers to lifestyles and judgments of taste that permeate certain social strata of contemporary society.

The not simple contrast of these and many others ways of conceiving the concept of culture would already be a reason for a long work. The interest here is only to emphasize that the focus of our argument is the notion of *cultural production,* an attempt to problematize the critique of bourgeois culture as it appeared in the first generation of the Frankfurt School. To this end, as well as the proposition above about a late transitional capitalism, we now propose to talk, instead of postmodernism, of a "post-culture industry"

---

[169] Eagleton, *The Idea*, 32.
[170] See, for example: Pierre Bourdieu, *O Poder Simbólico* (Rio de Janeiro: Bertrand Brasil, 2000).

as a concept that logically would follows from our central thesis regarding the prominence of the immaterial labor.[171]

We agree with Vercellone regarding the fact that concepts such as post-Fordism and Toyotism are insufficient for an understanding of the contemporary transformations.[172] On the other hand, our hypothesis is that the concept of late capitalism continues to be more adequate than that of cognitive capitalism. As for those who generally share the idea that we live in a post-industrial society and that labor in the modern sense is no longer the main source of wealth, two lines of argument stand out: a) that it exists today a primacy of technoscience; b) that *savoir*/knowledge is the main productive force. The hypothesis that we present is that *savoir* as producer of wealth must be problematized *as something that is constituted in the sphere of culture,* which is an object of critique that can elucidate both the effective content of immaterial labor and a new type of capital accumulation.

We consider that the fundamental question continues to be the understanding and critique of the capitalist mode of production, but at the same time we believe that Gorz's proposition that we witness different forms of production, which we can consider coexisting modes of production:

> We are going through a period in which many modes of production coexist. Modern capitalism, centered on the valorization of large masses of material fixed capital, is increasingly being replaced by a postmodern capitalism centered on the valorization of a so-called immaterial capital, also qualified as "human capital," "knowledge capital" or "intelligence capital."[173]

What is effectively new in this historical configuration, in our understanding, is not only the immaterial labor, but what we understand to be a process of aestheticization of wealth that goes beyond, even, the findings undertaken by the first theorists of postmodernism and the theorists of cognitive capitalism. For the former, the very concepts of capitalism and mode of production are a meta-narrative, non-existent as a historical totality. For the second, with the emphasis placed on knowledge, the aestheticization of the economic emerges as a subsidiary thesis of the main which is the

---

[171] Our intention is not simply to reject the concept of postmodernism as inadequate to characterize the cultural transformations of contemporary society, on the contrary, we see it as pertinent in the type of approach proposed by Jameson. What we intend to express here is the transition from industry to post-industry also in the cultural sphere, which is the very meaning we attribute to the concept of immaterial labor.

[172] Carlo Vercellone, "From Formal Subsumption to General Intellect: Elements for a Marxist Reading of the Thesis of Cognitive Capitalism." *Historical Materialism*, Vol. 15, no 1, (2007 b): 14.

[173] Gorz, *O Imaterial*, 15.

centrality of *savoir*. As we see, for example, in one of the definitions of the immaterial given by Lazzarato:

> On the other hand, considered to be the activity that produces the "cultural content" of the commodity, immaterial labor involves a range of activities that are not normally recognized as "labor" – in other words, the types of activities involved in setting and setting standards. artistic and cultural trends, fashions, tastes, consumption patterns, and, more strategically, public opinion. Once the privileged domain of the bourgeoisie and its children, these activities have since the late 1970s become the domain of what we have defined as "mass intellectuality".[174]

Lazzarato is referring to what he calls the informational and cultural content of the commodity. We have seen that the cognitive capitalism thesis clearly emphasizes the dimension of informational content, but, as we have already announced in Chapter 2, what does this second aspect, that of cultural content, actually refer to? We understand that its explanation may lead us to a better understanding of how wealth begins to be constituted in a totally different way. The comparisons made between the concepts of late capitalism and cognitive capitalism provided us with different elements for the central formulation of the thesis defended here: in late transition capitalism, the substance of wealth becomes effective in the aesthetic-cultural sphere. We see in the analysis of Ruy Fausto about the *Grundrisse* an analysis that seems to reinforce this thesis:

> Wealth is no longer produced by labor, but by non-labor. This in a double sense. First, material wealth is no longer essentially dependent on labor. Secondly, wealth becomes essentially science (art, etc.) and this is produced in non-labor time. So, the substance of wealth is no longer labor, but non-labor.[175]

We postulate that the forms of social domination that made possible the emergence of the first conceptions of late capitalism are still present, although central aspects of the historical basis that made them possible are radically changing. We refer mainly to late capitalism as thought by Adorno and Horkheimer. At the same time, those forms of domination are not exclusive to Jameson's conception of late capitalism, but are incorporated into it, in its central aspects, insofar as postmodernity is the realization of a new stage of capitalist domination.

---

[174] Maurizio Lazzarato, "Immaterial Labor," in *Radical Thought in Italy*, ed Michael Hardt and Paolo Virno, (Minneapolis: University of Minnesota Press, 1996), 133.
[175] Ruy Fausto, "A 'Pós-Grande Indústria' nos *Grundrisse* (e Para Além Deles)", *Lua Nova*, no 19 (novembro 1989): 63.

The advent of immaterial labor is the support point of a new stage of the capitalist mode of production, but it is at the same time the real and epistemological substratum of modern domination that is even more present in it. We affirm at the end of the third chapter that there are at least three aspects of the original formulation of late capitalism that have not lost their historical meaning: the exacerbation of instrumental rationality, the difficulty of dissociating the political and the economic, and the transformation of culture in commodity. In this latter aspect, the consequence is the non-exhaustion of the concept of reification as a decisive category for an understanding of a typically capitalist way of social domination.

The definition of the immaterial with which we have dealt so far posits it fundamentally as that activity that concerns the role of *savoir* and knowledge in its constitution. This *savoir*, as we have seen, is non-formalizable, consisting of learning and qualifications that are formed in everyday experiences, which permeates the attributes of creativity, imagination, initiative, discernment, cooperation, communication skills, etc. These are qualifications that, among others, would form what immaterial theorists call general intellect – the basis of the new productivity.

Our hypothesis is that such characteristics, which make up productive *savoir,* are essentially cultural. The subjectivity that produces wealth in immaterial terms is formed in the cultural sphere in a double sense, in that of the *savoirs* apprehended in everyday life, in artistic, educational, religious activities, etc., and in the aestheticization of market production, that is, in the way in which the image, the taste and the symbolic attributes come to represent the main aspect of the production itself. This second aspect is hardly new; it was already present in the work of Guy Debord[176] and is relevant to Fredric Jameson's theory of postmodernity. Postmodernity, as this author understands it, is not totally incompatible with some of the main theses regarding the immaterial. We understand that the hypothesis of the immaterial can be seen as a necessary development for Jameson's thesis, which, in our view, did not explore a decisive aspect of the current mutation of capitalism: the intertwining between culture and labor.[177] Although he has shown the way in which culture and economy join in late capitalism, Jameson does not show the way in which this culture is not only marketable,

---

[176] See: Guy Debord, *A Sociedade do Espetáculo* (Rio de Janeiro: Contraponto, 1998).

[177] The emphasis by Jameson and other authors on the inseparability of market and culture does not represent the same thing, therefore, as the inseparability of labor and culture. What we are proposing is to theoretically explore a path already opened by him, but not sufficiently addressed in a sociological perspective.

but at the same time labor in an immaterial sense, and, therefore, the basis of the wealth produced today in the world capitalism.

In the authors we examined regarding the concept of cognitive capitalism, we noticed that their arguments about knowledge as the main productive force do not sufficiently clear what is the cultural content of the immaterial. We refer, it is worth insisting, that for them knowledge is not just that which is formed in universities and research institutes, different from the emphasis of Bell and Castells, but the *savoir* that is socially constructed as collective intelligence. Although they correctly point to the sphere of non-labor time as the one that deserves to be better understood today, they do not make it sufficiently explicit as a sphere of cultural production.

In our initial approach, we noticed that immaterial labor is the result of a problematization regarding the separation between the production of value and the production of wealth. The problem arises as a direct reference to labor time, that is, in late capitalism general social labor, abstract labor, measurable in units of time, can no longer explain how the current stage of capitalist accumulation is taking shape. This labor, the center of Marxian thought, is being replaced by knowledge incorporated in the activity of immaterial labor, constituting itself as a form of value-knowledge. The insistence of cognitive capitalism theorists is that this knowledge, as *savoir*, is acquired outside labor time, as we saw earlier, that is, as externalities. Free time becomes a time for human capital formation, therefore, using the same economic rationality as labor time, making the distinction between the two spheres immensely difficult.

Let us think about this free time or non-labor time. In the first place, the formation of the so-called human capital, which tends to replace the figure of the wage worker, depends directly on what individuals do outside their labor hours: study, take improvement courses, learn a foreign language, play sports, doing volunteer work, investing in personal appearance, care, being communicative and sociable in leisure time, having tourist experiences, acquiring culinary knowledge, and so on. In addition to those characteristics of an even more primary socialization, such as the willingness to collaborate with the company, see it as a team, a collaborative group, an entity to which the worker must dedicate himself as if it were an extension of his home:

> Post-Fordist workers, on the contrary, must enter the production process with all the cultural baggage they acquired in games, team sports, fights, disputes, musical and theatrical activities, etc. It is in these activities outside of work that his vivacity, his capacity for improvisation and cooperation are developed. It is their vernacular knowledge that the post-Fordist enterprise puts to work and exploits. Yann Moulier-Boutang calls 'second degree

exploitation' this subsumption to capital of collective labor as living labor, and not as the power of science and machines.[178]

Everyday culture! But free time is also the time of postmodern culture, therefore, the time of consumption. Inside and outside labor time, the world of commodities has fundamentally become image, aesthetic apprehension of reality. This time of consumption can no longer be identified only with the time of the *flaneur*, the passerby and the crowd, as Walter Benjamin said in his analysis of modernity, of Baudelaire's Paris.[179] The daily life outside the factory, which was already a time of consumption for the modern individual, is acquiring another meaning in the current phase of late capitalism. Even the image of the *shopping center* as a modern temple of consumption began to find an alternative, one that represents the vertiginous growth of consumption through the network, the use of the internet and tele-delivery services as a new consumption format that is changing the very way of apprehending the experience of modernity.

The reified consciousness of postmodernity is itself a producer of wealth. This consciousness is no longer just a form of reproduction, a distorted reflection of a reality that is also false. Human relations are becoming guided by the logic of economic rationality and by the possession of symbols or access, in an unmatched proportion to the previous stages of capitalism, because now they are no longer distinguished from the logic previously attributed only to the economic sphere. The culture industry changes its meaning inasmuch as the production of the images is more important than the material goods. In defending a concept of cultural capitalism Rifkin says:

> Evidence is everywhere. The cultural industries – a term coined by German sociologists Theodor Adorno and Max Horkheimer in the 1930s – are the fastest growing sector of the global economy. Film, radio, television, record companies, global tourism, shopping malls, leisure centers, theme cities, theme parks, fashion, cuisine, professional sports and games, gambling, physical fitness and the simulated worlds and virtual realities of cyberspace are the frontline of commercial fields in the Age of Access.[180]

But as industrial production ceases to be the core of late capitalism, we understand that the concept of culture industry must also be thought of in other terms. We can still speak of capitalism, among other reasons, because

---

[178] Gorz, *O Imaterial*, 19.
[179] Walter Benjamin, *Textos de Sociologia,* editado por Flávio Kothe, (São Paulo: Ática, 1985a).
[180] Rifkin, *A Era do Acesso*, 113.

the world continues to be dominated by the production of commodities, but the way in which these commodities are produced has changed radically. Increasingly, they tend to present themselves, in their form, as dematerialized goods, as are electronic devices, today located as the epicenter of consumption in the world. The prominence of the immaterial is given on the one hand, by the use of science and technology in production, something that had already been predicted by Marx in the *Grundrisse,* but on the other hand, by a modification of the role of culture, made inseparable from the economy. The value of commodities is starting to have, necessarily, an aesthetic and symbolic content, which no longer refers to abstract labor.

The aesthetic dimension is not only added to the value of the commodity but becomes its principal component. At the same time, the commodity workforce is only valued to the extent that it also incorporates this symbolic and aesthetic dimension. Some authors call this the formation of human capital, but we understand it as a set of cultural attributes, since the *savoir* mobilized by the worker refers to a subjectivity that is hardly distinguishable from the very act of producing symbolic content, including its own labor force.

The historical impetus for this perception of the aesthetic in contemporary social theory were Adorno and Horkheimer, whose critique of capitalism we sketched in the third chapter. The cultural phenomena most studied by Frankfurtians were undoubtedly music and cinema. Both represented the procedure par excellence of technical rationalization. Fordist procedures for standardizing goods were exemplarily applied both to the music production of the 1940s and to those that followed, and to cinema even more so. Hollywood films produced in series endorsed a certain historic moment in the movement of commodity. The problem was that the film was not just any consumer good, but human subjectivity led directly to the impossibility of reflection. The worker became an appendage of the machine even when away from it. It is evident that instrumental rationality also began to encompass other forms of cultural production: architecture, literature, photography and the publishing market of newspapers and magazines. In all of Adorno's theorizing of the culture industry there is solid grounding in Marxian categories, including the labor theory of value. It is precisely these more clearly Marxian aspects that will be emphasized by Fredric Jameson to show that what from the 1970s onwards came to be called postmodernity could still be understood by the categories developed in the Adornian negative dialectic, especially the categories of totality and mode of production.

We saw earlier in what way postmodernism is for Jameson the cultural logic of late capitalism. The music, cinema, literature, and architecture that had been criticized by Adorno changed completely with postmodernity. For Jameson what has been produced in literature, cinema, video, architecture, music, and other aesthetic manifestations over the last three decades has become something completely indistinguishable from market. The aesthetic was incorporated into the very mechanisms of the mode of production in its new stage. Postmodernism is thus the cultural dominant of this new stage in which the image takes precedence over narrative and becomes the "great commodity":

> Surely what characterizes postmodernity in the cultural sphere is the suppression of everything outside commercial culture, its absorption of all forms of art high and low, along with image production itself. The image is the commodity today, and that is why it is vain to expect a negation of the logic of commodity production from it, that is why, finally, all beauty today is meretricious and the appeal to it by contemporary pseudo-aestheticism is an ideological manoeuvre and not a creative resource.[181]

Jameson's descriptions of culture in postmodernity hardly differ from what cognitive capitalism theorists say about the cultural aspect of the commodity produced by immaterial labor. We are talking about how the commodity is only valued, or produces wealth, when there is an aesthetic component in its production. In late capitalism, the culture industry exists and has ceased to exist, just like other industries. It exists in part in its modern form, still Fordist, but is gradually transforming itself into a post-culture industry. The cultural transformations of the last thirty-five years are so intense and profound that even some of the characteristics of so-called postmodernism seem to be changing. We can refer to the inseparability between culture and immaterial labor when we take the classic models of analysis of cultural production, such as television, cinema, and music.

We said above that television and cinema, as thought by Adorno between the 1940s and 1960s, changed in terms of their own model. At that historical moment, there was not only a popularization of the television set itself, but there was, as until very recently, the production of standardized series and films in terms of their aesthetic form and narrative structure. Films and series were produced as if they were electric mixers. With postmodernism we see changes in this structure. Firstly, we have a change in the aesthetic form itself with the emergence of what Jameson called nostalgia films. In this genre of film, which began to have an impact from the end of the 1970s onwards, we perceive all the characteristics of

---

[181] Jameson, *The Cultural Turn*, 135.

postmodernism: the absence of the new, the quotation, the pastiche, the elaboration of a schizophrenic temporality.[182]

We have, on the other hand, the massive development of video, considered by Jameson the art pattern of postmodernity. Video changes not only the course of cinema history, but the very spatiality and everyday meaning of movie theaters, as people watch their films at home on VCR, and then on DVD, which allows a direct control over the movie's progress. It is possible to resume a point from it, advance and jump. The one who watches is already less passive about the work that his eyes observe. But in the 1980s we also had a properly aesthetic change in terms of video, insofar as it has the characteristic of lasting less time, fifteen or twenty minutes, and this is exemplary in the phenomenon of the video clip, a sequence of images and songs that last just a few minutes. Here we have a change in the temporality of the narrative.

Both cinema and television are undergoing historical transformations that encompass the broad field of the image and that are confused at the same time with the so-called immaterial labor. When we previously analyzed the active role played by the consumer in immaterial production, we were referring to something that also permeates the television model that is being constituted in the first decade of the 21st century. A considerable portion of the so-called *reality-shows,* for example, develop from the intervention of the spectator in the plot that unfolds. Every day and every week millions of viewers participate by phone or over the internet in the unraveling of the narrative. But this occurs in a broad sense of television programming. There are practically no television programs without the "direct participation" of the viewer: sports, religious, variety programs, news programs, talk shows, etc. In Brazil, even the script of telenovelas depends on how the audience follows the plot, and it has become increasingly common for authors to alter the original text of their fiction as a result of the public's liking for this or that character and their tele-dramaturgical destiny.

We see, in this way, that the consumer participates and decides on how the television commodity will be presented, instead of simply watching it. And it does so as in the economy of the immaterial it does with automobiles, refrigerators, and clothes. What the Sociology of Work calls Toyotist production we do not believe to be just a nomenclature. Post-Fordism, even though it may exist concomitantly with other production models, is also present in the audiovisual post-industry. Here we have a clear example of how subjectivity is not only a passive and reified receiver, but its reification

---

[182] See: Jameson, *Pós-Modernismo.*

implies that the individual participates fully and completely in the production process. The individual, while enjoying his free time in front of the television set, at the same time participates in the production of the television commodity that distracts him. Cultural production, immaterial labor, production of wealth!

If in the classic period of the culture industry, individuals left the cinema with a feeling of passion or hatred for the character in the film, he can now, in a way, express his anger, for example, taking his cell phone and sending an SMS to the specific number of that program. This interactivity, which also has a great deal of artificiality, but which cannot be overlooked in terms of its active role, that is, of a consumer who determines what will be produced, is only possible because of the transforming role that communications play in the late capitalism, as Bell, Castells, Rifkin, and others pointed out.

Transformations in the sphere of communications are directly contributing to the solidification of the image as the commodity par excellence of advanced capitalism. We are facing phenomena that did not even exist when Jameson drafted his book on postmodernity in 1990. The transformations that are taking place are so intense within a decade that what seems to us to be new can be obsolete today. Video images today are no longer limited in terms of their production to a small group of specialized technicians in cinema, and their consumption occurs in diverse ways, which also involve the new spatiality in which we live.

One of the recent phenomena is the production of images through portable digital cameras and cell phones. Images of the most diverse types captured in everyday life are placed on sites such as *You Tube,* or simply posted on blogs or personal pages that can and are accessed by millions of people around the world. This production of images that can be seen as a kind of collectively produced *savoir* is in line with what cognitive capitalism theorists think. It is a *savoir* that resists being transformed into a commodity, but at the same, in our understanding, they express the reification of culture. Images are also present in everyday life as commodity and exacerbation of the culture industry, as productive consumption, immaterial labor.

The image of a commodity today corresponds to a more than considerable part of its value. This makes activities related to photography, audiovisual techniques, design, and advertising become the core of capitalist production itself. But this predominance of the image does not exclude the manifestation of a similar phenomenon in other branches of the "post-culture industry." Immaterial labor is the formation of consumer taste and at the same time the possibility of apprehending certain trends already existing in the market:

> The particularity of the commodity produced by immaterial labor (its use value being essentially its informational and cultural content) consists in the fact that it is not destroyed in the act of consumption, but that it expands, transforms, creates the ideological and cultural environment of the consumer. It does not reproduce the physical capacity of the workforce; it transforms its user.[183]

In the field of music, for example, we understand that the great transformation we are going through does not necessarily have to be sought in the scope of aesthetic form. Jameson at times showed the impossibility of distinguishing high culture and mass culture, since numerous contemporary musical manifestations showed the impossibility of distinguishing between the two spheres in terms of their aesthetic qualification.[184] We see, however, that the thesis regarding the coexistence of different modes of production can be found in contemporary musicality, expressing our hypothesis about the expression "post-culture industry."

On the one hand, it is quite evident that the classic model of the culture industry, in terms of music, is present in the daily lives of people anywhere in the world. All we need to do is listen (through the network) to the most popular radio stations in Paris, Berlin, New York, and compare with any Brazilian city to observe the same phenomenon, pointed out by Adorno more than half a century ago as regression in hearing. On the other hand, the way of listening to music is changing and this change is so profound that it brings up another theme dear to thinkers of the immaterial, which is copyright.[185]

We know that, just like the old vinyl record, the CD disc format has its days numbered and this has been announced for several years. What was previously thought of as a miniaturization of material goods is now much more than that, as it tends to become a dematerialization of the very vehicle with which music is heard (a phenomenon that is already occurring with the television set and tends to intensify in the coming years). In the case of

---

[183] Corsani, Antonella, Maurizio Lazzarato, et Antonio Negri, *Le Bassin du travail immatériel (BTI) dans la Métropole Parisienne* (Paris: L'Harmattan, 1996), 82.

[184] Jameson, *Pós-Modernismo*, 88.

[185] About the issue of intellectual property see, for example: Barbrook, Richard. "A regulamentação da liberdade: liberdade de expressão, liberdade de comércio e liberdade de dádiva na rede". In *Capitalismo Cognitivo*, ed. Cocco, Giuseppe; Alexander Patez Galvão; e Gerardo Silva (Rio de Janeiro: DP & A, 2003), 133-50.

music prevail, even among the "popular layers," the use of iPod, mp3, mp4, 3G cell phones, and so on, which continues have been modified and innovated. The use of such devices also represents changes in human cognition, in the form of sociability and insertion in labor relationships. In human resource agency forms, for example, the email address and cell phone number appear as mandatory fields to be filled in. But, returning to the case of music, we can see that often the material substrate of production does not even exist.

Another phenomenon of the "post-culture industry" is the production of music directly using the computer, often without the use of a single musical instrument. Through minimal technological resources made available by a computer and software, "instrumental" songs are "composed" and the way to disseminate them, such as video images, is by placing them on the internet, in most cases for free. We understand that the great phonographic industry, a model par excellence of the culture industry, now not only coexists with a dematerialization of its product, the record, but the even more important transformation is that today we "download" most of the songs on our personal computer and records we want to listen to without directly paying a penny for it. In this case, we have a good example of a cultural object that resists expressing itself as a commodity, although no less subject to reification.

Immaterial labor, when referring to a type of intertwining between production and consumption that could not be visualized in this way in the previous phase of capitalism, is at the same time, and contradictorily, the transformation of life itself into a commodity, in a sense possibly much broader than that addressed in all contemporary theses on reification. Immaterial labor is shown especially in fashion and advertising, through the formation of consumers taste and imagination; it forms the cultural and symbolic environment where consumption is not limited to the mere use of commodity.

In this case, immaterial labor is ideologically identified with the same functions historically fulfilled by the culture industry. One of the differences between the culture industry of past decades and the present is that the so-called fragmentation of postmodernity no longer advertises a preconceived commodity that will later form a consumer market. It is this market in its fragmentation that interacts with the productive sphere, and in this case, the celebrated cultural differences of late modernity become one of the most promising branches of consumption. In the first years of the 21st century, ecological appeals and products aimed at queer people, for example, represent a significant share of the market.

One of the objections to the existence of the immaterial is the observation that all advertising, including on the internet, has a material substrate. As we have already said, this objection is due to a certain misunderstanding as to what immaterial labor is. First, this objection, while partially true, fails to deny that commodities are dematerializing, either in the form of miniaturization or in substituting possession for access, but mainly when they see the immaterial fundamentally as the commodity itself, and not as *an activity*. Advertising, as an immaterial activity, tends to represent the largest share of value added to a commodity, whether material or not. Its role is essentially cultural, that is, to shape the consumer's taste and at the same time apprehend it, in its diversity and multiplicity, to make it a commodity. In a late transitional capitalism, advertising aims to form a social subjectivity that finds its purpose in consumption. It is no longer a question of creating new needs for the proletariat to consume, it is a question of creating symbols and images without which sociability itself is unfeasible; the search for such symbols begins to move increasingly towards access at the expense of material possession.

The way in which taste and aesthetics in contemporary society establish new social hierarchies is also something that we cannot ignore. As we will see in the next chapter, the fact that it is no longer possible to speak of the proletariat today as in a previous moment of capitalism does not mean that there are no more classes, much less social stratification.

We saw above how seemingly paradoxical capitalism is at the present time. We start from the hypothesis that labor time is no longer the fundamental constituent of value and that value, like social wealth, is rapidly being constructed by something other than abstract labor. For some it is the *savoir*. In our view, it is the subjectivity forged by the cultural sphere. Paradoxical in this case is that what is referred to as what happens outside labor time has an emancipatory potential, as Gorz says, if seen as mass intelligentsia. But it is at the same time, as we understand it, a new type of reification, in which human life, more than in previous stages of capitalism, is becoming appropriated by capital. In the next chapter we will try to analyze other dimensions of this contradiction.

CHAPTER 7

THE OLD DOMINATION
AND THE NEW EXPLOITATION

In our approach that privileges the concept of late capitalism as well as in that of cognitive capitalism, it is evident that the prominence of immaterial labor did not eliminate the forms of social domination engendered by modernity but deepened them. Throughout the previous chapters, when we showed that the ongoing transformations largely refer to a change in human subjectivity, we also point to the fact that this new subjectivity was not able to get rid of that model of domination of nature, based on an instrumental rationality, and which marked the understanding of capitalism of the first generation of critical theorists of the Frankfurt School.

Just as different generations of Frankfurtians expressed different conceptions of late capitalism, their conceptions of domination are also change. In our view, Adorno's theory of domination continues to be adequate for the understanding of a late transitional capitalism, however, the new historical elements posed by immaterial labor require not only a new look at what this author called the culture industry, but also a new look at the way in which the forms of social domination of modernity not only remain in postmodernity but also begin to acquire a new meaning.

We mentioned earlier that the critique of domination throughout the development of industrial and Fordist society, with a strong emphasis from the first Critical Theory, had already shifted its epicenter from the idea of domination as exploitation, as class domination. What we are calling late capitalism is precisely the proposition of a new concept of domination that aims to put new elements on the original conception of Theodor W. Adorno. It seems plausible to suggest that in a post-industrial society, an expression of an even more advanced phase of this late capitalism, domination should also be thought through epistemological and normative parameters that are not limited to the framework of Marxian categories. But, in claiming a Critical Theory, we are not postulating the abandonment of Marx's thought, but the incorporation of his theses on class domination as one of the manifestations of a domination whose central axis continues to be, in our understanding, the so-called instrumental rationality.

Thinking about the status of domination in the current stage of capitalism requires, at the same time, that we continue to think about the historical destiny of the proletariat, and its very concept. But it also requires that we not belittle contributions of contemporary social theory that are not exactly affiliated with Marxism, as the Frankfurtian tradition itself did by incorporating the Weberian critique of modern rationality. To what extent in the current phase of capitalism is the domination of modernity expressed in a new way? In what sense did the figure of the proletariat actually disappear or was it replaced by an exploited class based on immaterial labor? What is the effective relationship between domination and wealth-producing culture?

For Adorno as well as for Horkheimer and Marcuse, it is the subjectivity of the modern individual, especially that of the proletariat, which condenses the need for a new theory of domination against that of 19th century Marxism. Labor, contrary to what Lukács had conceived, ceases to be the potentially emancipatory space in which the proletariat acquired a "disalienated" and transforming self-consciousness. Culture, transposed to everyday life as mass culture, not only repeats the instrumental model that already exists in Fordist factories, but also becomes a privileged instance for the reproduction of bourgeois ideology and thought. Where is the limit of this thought for the understanding of domination and culture in the age of the immaterial?

In globalized capitalism, in late capitalism, the main characteristic of the predominant form of subjectivity is that it is no longer just a kind of receptacle of bourgeois reified consciousness, and therefore of heteronomous thinking. The so-called heteronomy manifests itself today in a way that was not perceptible in previous stages of capitalism, since subjectivity becomes active, not exactly in the sense of German idealism, but through a new form of schematism, as already proposed by Adorno, only that now as a directly productive subjectivity. Consciousness no longer posits itself as a sphere of reproduction, but directly as a sphere of production.

It is in this specific sense that the notion of reification needs to be thought of in terms other than that of Lukács and Adorno.[186] At the same

---

[186] We understand Honneth's recent attempts to rethink the concept of reification in the context of Critical Theory to be extremely significant, but it seems to us that his book only reopens the debate on a concept that seemed already forgotten by theory, and that he puts elements for future developments regarding the ideas that we are presenting here in this book. See: Axel Honneth, *Reification: A new look at an old idea* (New York: Oxford University Press, 2008).

time that this "new subjectivity" continues to function in the molds of an instrumental rationality, and because of the relevance of the latter, the role it plays in the general mechanisms of capital accumulation and production of wealth is completely different. As we will see next, the thinkers of *Multitudes* start from the concept of biopolitics to explain the new ways of domination. Our purpose is to show that from the distinction that we suggested in the previous chapter between knowledge/*savoir* and culture, we can think about this new stage of capitalist domination from the point of view of the Adornian categories of totality and not identity, unlike the appropriations derived from poststructuralism.

As oblivious as Adorno to the way in which capitalist domination is manifested in the specific sphere of labor,[187] Habermas understands it from an epistemological information completely different from that of Adorno. Domination is now understood as the impossibility of free speech acts, as an obstacle to understanding, as pathologies of modernity. It becomes emphatic, therefore, in the context of the political debate about democracy. While moving away from the dialectical model visible in Marx, Lukács and Adorno, Habermas opens the way to understanding a central dimension of domination in contemporary society; one that refers to the sphere of culture in the sense of a sphere in which symbolic patterns of identity are shared, and therefore, contributing decisively to the ongoing debates on ethnic, gender and different minority movements.

We saw in previous chapters of our exposition that one of the problems of strong implication in our hypothesis regarding the inseparability between cultural production and immaterial labor is its polemics with the well-known conception of Habermas and Gorz about the concept of the lifeworld. Such a concept, as we have shown, has been shown to be incompatible with the current state of capitalist domination. In Gorz's work, the distinction between economic rationality, associated with the idea of modern labor, and the lifeworld, is quite emphatic in the works that correspond to a second phase of his intellectual production, that is, in works before *O Imaterial*.[188]

For Gorz, in these works, all labor guided by economic rationality is an expression of heteronomy and domination. It is thus assumed that the lifeworld, external to labor, warrants the possibility of forms of human

---

[187] Among the many critiques made to Frankfurtian thought, one of them, and which we consider very relevant, is that in their different historical moments these thinkers do not develop specific reflections on the sphere of labor and its transformations in contemporary society. We understand that this kind of "labor category analysis deficit" characterizes the three generations of Frankfurtians mentioned here.
[188] See: Camargo, "Capitalism."

sociability not taken by domination embodied in economic rationality. Gorz's references in this regard are frequent:

> Including leisure in the field of economics and saying that its extension will generate new economic activities is a paradoxical way of hiding the issue. Leisure activities, in fact, have an inverse rationality to that of economic activities: they are not producers, but consumers of available time; they aim not to gain time, but to spend it. They correspond to the time of celebration, of prodigality, of free activity that has no other purpose than its own. In short, time that is useless, that is not a means to any other end; instrumental rationality categories (efficacy, yield, performance) are inapplicable to leisure activities; if they were, there would be an elevated risk of perverting them.[189]

As we have seen, it is a form of understanding like that of Habermas, whose theory of communicative action is based on the attempt to verify, theoretically and empirically, that instrumental and strategic reason finds its limits in a society in which the democratic institutions of modernity, and the new social movements, manifest the emancipatory potential of modernity. For Gorz, it is the free time and labor with no economic purpose that prove to be impermeable to systemic rationality. In both forms of understanding, which in no way resemble the dialectic of totality, the everyday, the lived, and the sphere of culture, represent spheres resistant to domination. What we tried to show in the two previous chapters shows the opposite path to this thesis.

Immaterial labor, as an expression of a new moment in contemporary culture, by constituting itself precisely in everyday experiences, in spaces and temporalities outside labor (in an industrial sense), reveals a new stage of Adorno's concept of domination. Insofar as social relations continue to be, until the present, capitalist relations, immaterial labor points to a new expression of the apparently already aged instrumental rationality, in the form of an extension of modern domination. Its manifestation becomes clear, as shown in Chapter 6, in the maintenance and transformation of the culture industry, but, more than that, in a kind of "total mobilization", in which the body, language and life themselves become the manifestation of a new stage, distinct from the beginning of modern philosophy, called heteronomy:

> In order to expose as generally as possible what accompanies this "total mobilization", we will say that, for many, it is the set of determinations of their own life as the relational center that can be summoned; to this extent,

---

[189] Gorz, *Metamorfoses do Trabalho*, 17.

it is the whole of lifetime that becomes virtually subject to control and requested by the productive apparatus. To put it another way: the system of domination/exploitation becomes integrally biopolitical.[190]

The form of domination on which immaterial labor rests makes gestures more apparently innocent on the basis of productivity. The people of contemporary society have transformed their non-labor time into support for a new stage of accumulation. Let us remember that what defines immaterial labor are cooperative, informational, and communicative activities, in which the creative and intellectual aspects of human activity stand out. Immaterial labor is that type of activity that is *always inseparable from a component of "savoir" that is formed mainly in the time and space of non-work,* including the sphere of consumption.

Let us recover once more the ramifications of this definition. The concept of cooperation, for example, refers to a set of behaviors that would be present both in the actual manufacturing and business activity, situated in the workspace itself, and outside it, as a positive externality,[191] which would form the so-called "mass intelligentsia." Authors who approach the concept of post-Fordism also call it the verticalization of labor relations, in which the hierarchical and spatial compartmentalization of the Fordist model are replaced by forms of labor as the worker acts together and simultaneously with others. In contemporary companies, this principle of spatiality is quite visible when we see dozens of workers with their desks lined up, without partitions that separate them and where they interact all the time.

This cooperation that takes place within the company is based on the principle of worker adherence to the activities to be developed. The company is no longer, ideologically, the place of mere fulfillment of tasks alienated from the beginning. The individual must identify with it, "wear the shirt" of the company and always be ready to collaborate with colleagues and superiors. This cooperation concerns, therefore, the mobilization of a subjectivity, which includes the body, in favor of a greater aim, the cause of the company, the cause of capital. We are thus talking about something that goes beyond the appropriation of surplus labor and the production of surplus value, and which is far beyond the classical category of alienation. The domination that appears there, and it seems to us undeniable to be a new characteristic of capitalist companies, ultimately depends on an appropriation of the worker's own life, who now has the "freedom to cooperate." The

---

[190] Bernard Aspe et Muriel Combes, « Revenu garanti et biopolitique », *Multitudes* (Octobre, 2004). https://www.multitudes.net/revenu-garanti-et-biopolitiique/
[191] Moulier-Boutang, *Le Capitalisme*, 39.

principle of instrumental rationality is outlined there through a new characteristic that only became feasible with the advent of immaterial labor.

The other pole of cooperation, the one made possible by the advent of the network society, by the use of computers and the internet not only in production, but in the broad dimension of contemporary sociability, refers to the fact that the abstract multiplicity of brains that produce diffused knowledge in society as a whole manifest the possibility of cooperating in the creation of new knowledge that is expressed in the very domain of the informational sphere, that is, when, for example, *software* is created or improved within the scope of open source. The knowledge of different individuals collaborates by bringing together different brains. For most thinkers of cognitive capitalism, this is the point of support for what they call knowledge/*savoir* communism,[192] and Lazzarato and Negri goes as far as to say that such elements already exist in us present as *potentially* communist society.[193]

The communicational activities that underlie immaterial labor, emphasized by all theorists of post-industrial society, can hardly be understood today in the Habermasian sense of speech acts aimed at understanding. The use of language in the daily flow of the information society not only seems distant from a communication free of economic rationality but is also the basis of the new productivity. We saw in our approach to culture that communicational processes serve to form and apprehend the taste of consumers, and more than that, the reification embodied in the consumption of images is at the same time a consumption of a semiotic production disseminated by the various media. Communication is thus a formative aspect of capital, but also part of the cultural sphere:

> This demonstrates that a superficial concept, that of communication, was suddenly endowed with a new cultural dimension: a communicational signifier acquired a more properly cultural meaning or significance. In this way, postulating the expansion of communication networks ends up surreptitiously transforming itself into a position on the new world culture.[194]

On the other hand, everyday communication, contextualized in the lifeworld, which also affects the content of immaterial labor, is extremely far from the spontaneity of speech acts. One of the requirements placed on the cognitive worker is the ability of workers to communicate with customers, with co-workers, with superiors, in the most different situations,

---

[192] Gorz, *O Imaterial*, 59.
[193] Lazzarato and Negri, *Trabalho Imaterial*, 41.
[194] Jameson, *A Cultura do Dinheiro* (Petrópolis: Vozes, 2001a), 45.

even outside the company environment. The human capital thesis only endorses this idea that knowing how to communicate means knowing how to use language, or use it strategically, to keep certain symbolic patterns intact that labor as in a game of strict rules. Knowing how to behave and communicate outside the work environment is just as important as the opposite.

Domination would be a colonization of the lifeworld by the system, if the rules that govern the lifeworld were not, as they are, themselves bearers of a rationality that is absorbed by the system. This rationality is not new in terms of its conceptual content, the cynicism, the dissimulation, the lie, the performance. The goods produced by immaterial labor, whose main content is symbolic, are the expression of a new type of reification, of the subject's inability to self-reflect, and it is in this sense that the postulation of knowledge/*savoir* as the main aspect of cognitive capitalism must be problematized. And it is also in this sense that the Habermasian theory, in our understanding, faces today not only epistemic but also historical limitations.

When contextualizing domination as something specific to critical theory of society, we also need to consider the recent contributions of Axel Honneth. But what is the relationship between Honneth's thought and the thesis of a capitalism that is understood by the centrality of immaterial labor? Firstly, it is necessary to remember that for Honneth, the notion of domination shifts to the philosophical problem of injustice, whose understanding starts, as for Habermas, from the concept of intersubjectivity, and then manifests itself as a struggle for recognition. Honneth's central focus becomes, in his most recent thinking, not the concepts of domination and power, nor exploitation, but injustice.

Honneth is concerned with showing the way in which certain pre-theoretical experiences, which precede the communicative action itself, lead individuals, in different circumstances of social life, to the almost intuitive perception of situations of disrespect, therefore of non-recognition, being there a plausible explanation for the very existence of different social movements, since disrespect refers to at least three different levels of human life.[195] Feelings of social disrespect do not, of course, refer only to the conflict between social classes, for as much as Habermas, Honneth can also be called a non-productivist. Its clear intention, however, is to recover the initial problems of Critical Theory for a new context, that is, those that concern the way in which the emancipatory will of individuals can be

---

[195] Josué Pereira da Silva, *Trabalho, Cidadania e Reconhecimento* (São Paulo: Annablume, 2008), 98.

understood, or, under what conditions it is possible. His explanation is that moral experiences are the ones that enable the triggering of a struggle for recognition. In fact, not exactly the moral conscience of disrespect, but intuitive notions of injustice that motivate the resistance action of individuals.

Honneth understands that forms of injustice are only understandable if at the same time we understand the historical and structural contextualization in which they manifest themselves, including in the sense of pathologies of capitalist society. Unlike Habermas, he points to the fact that the understanding of forms of disrespect cannot underestimate the role of labor as a dimension of human sociability, in this case, making a kind of self-critique of the very history of the Frankfurt School. However, this attention to the role of labor as a fundamental nucleus of expression of injustice seems to have not yet found, even in this author, a more effective study that encompasses, for example, the dimension and importance of immaterial labor in contemporary forms of sociability, as we have been trying to show so far.

It is possible to affirm that between the different conceptions of domination that mark the theorists who emphasize the concept of late capitalism and, on the other hand, the recent French tradition that claims the concept of cognitive capitalism, there is also the difference that the latter are concerned with explicitly from the idea of exploitation, in the sense of the Marxian tradition, even if to approach it through a recontextualization of biopower. Exploitation and biopower thus configure a conceptual pair that appears as a theoretical alternative to the different approaches to the concept of domination present in the critical theory of society. Such conceptions, however, do not seem to us to be totally excluding, insofar as they both start from the premise that even exploitation no longer has the same characteristics as those of industrial society.

Understanding capitalism as an economic system of domination was already visible in Marx. Marx refers not only to the way in which an individual dominates or exploits another individual, but refers to how the capitalist mode of production, as a historical totality, subtracts the freedom of individuals considering the abstract character of this system is highlighted.[196] Marx's thesis, as part of the Marxist tradition embodied it, tends to reduce domination to a simplified view of the exploitation of one class by another. The first generation of Critical Theory sought to dilute this simplification, while authors such as Gorz tried to show the very limitation of a concept of domination centered on the category of labor, taken as an anthropological concept, since economic rationality can subtract the

---

[196] Postone, *Time, Labor,* 31.

freedom of individuals even under historical conditions where the actual condition of exploitation is not visible. The discussions that took place throughout the 20th century regarding the nature of the Soviet State also expressed this problem regarding the relationship between domination and exploitation.

Once again, we are faced with our initial postulation about the distinction between mode of production and mode of distribution. Those who understand that the end of private property and the establishment of a planned economy will be the end of capitalist domination overlook the fact that, within the framework of an industrial mode of production, with its specific form of labor and rationality, domination tends to perpetuate itself in the form of heteronomous labor with forms of sociability associated with it. The fact that the concept of exploitation is insufficient to show the effective domination engendered by modernity does not mean that it does not exist, on the contrary, it becomes an even greater challenge to understand how the exploitation of labor is also changing from the emergence of immaterial labor.

It is in this sense that cognitive capitalism theorists speak of degree 2 self-exploitation and exploitation as correlated with the advent of immaterial labor. Capitalism tends to appropriate not only the labor time of others, but the worker's lifetime from the perspective of biopower. Moulier-Boutang refers to what he calls a system of exploitation of degree 2. A degree 1 exploitation is that which characterizes the labor relations of modern capitalism, and which evidently did not simply cease to exist, but it coexists at the same time with a type of exploitation that became even more important and central, the one that concerns the appropriation of collective labor, that is, of collective intelligence itself:

> And I will call exploitation of degree 2, a subsumption degree to the capital of collective labor as living labor and not as the power of science and machines. In order for the conditions of complex labor to unite complex living labor in the unity of the productive act and in the continuity of the valorization process, two things are necessary: a) that living labor be incorporated into the cycle of commodity circulation; b) that it be subsumed in the production process as living labor that resides as such, that is, fully alive throughout the operation, which is not the case with the entropic model of the conversion of muscular and nervous energy into a product or service.[197]

---

[197] Yann Moulier-Boutang, « La troisième transition du capitalisme: exode du travail productif et externalités », in *Vers Un Capitalisme Cognitif,* Ed Christian Azaïs; Antonella Corsani et Patrick Dieuaide (Paris: L'Harmattan, 2001), 140.

As we have seen, capital in its current phase increasingly tends to produce wealth not from labor time, but from a productive subjectivity. Even here, domination is visible as exploitation, although, in our understanding, in the form of private appropriation of knowledge. The new workers of late capitalism, by some authors called *cognitariate* and *pronetariat*, are exploited in two ways: in the still existing forms of wage labor, even when it is cognitive, and in the form of self-exploitation, while mobilizing a subjectivity that will result in capital's appropriation of its knowledge. André Gorz emphasizes that the advent of human capital is accompanied by new forms of exploitation. Even if it is no longer a direct extraction of surplus value, it is now a kind of self-exploitation:

> I have laid out for you two elements of an exploitation reset. The first is what YM Boutang calls "second degree exploitation" which we can consider as a form of "predation of externalities." It consists of companies valuing human capital, which they have never accumulated and which they therefore consider to be an integral part of their fixed capital [...]. The second, complementary element is what Combes and Aspe called "total mobilization," the title of a famous writing published by Ernest Junger in 1934. Through "total mobilization" the company does not only value "human fixed capital" of capabilities and competences, which is the results of production itself; it now directly explores the production of itself.[198]

To understand this new form of exploitation, it is necessary to remember another argumentative aspect that we are developing. The existence of a new stage of capitalism does not eliminate its coexistence with aspects of its previous stage. We realize that, to a considerable extent, central characteristics of Fordism and even Taylorism are still present in broad sectors of contemporary society, including the forms of labor organization. In this way, the extraction of surplus value, the intensification of labor, an increase in working hours, a reduction in wages, the extinction of labor rights, are present in the contemporary context and continue to be present as an integral part of what characterizes capital.

Both Gorz and other cognitive theorists emphasize the creativity and intellectual gifts of the immaterial worker. A considerable portion, perhaps even more quantitatively expressive of what we can call the new proletariat, develops so-called cognitive activities, such as the operation of computers, through extremely repetitive, rationalized forms of labor, limiting their intellectual expressiveness, the most solid example of which is a category

---

[198] André Gorz, « Économie de la connaissance, exploitation des savoirs », Entretien réalisé par Yann Moulier- Boutang et Carlo Vercellone. *Multitudes* 15, (juin 2004b), https://www.cairn.info/revue-multitudes-2004-1-page-205.htm

that grows every day in Brazil and in the world, which is that of call center operators. In this example, even the worker who is directly engaged in an activity that involves the use of intellectual and communicative abilities is completely limited in his creativity and expressiveness, not being substantially different from any worker of the Fordist era.

Although the prominence of the immaterial points to the logical possibility of reducing labor time, as already stated in the *Grundrisse,* and as André Gorz establishes as a banner of political struggle, we have no historical evidence that modern forms of labor exploitation have diminished with late capitalism. In many sectors of activity, which even deal directly with the concept of immaterial outlined here, such as teachers, bank employees, health workers, etc., the intensification of labor and even the extension of the working day is something quite visible. If the old forms of exploitation are being replaced by others, this does not mean that those have disappeared.

The way in which the direct exploitation of surplus value continues to be a visibly integral part of the present regime of accumulation serves as an elucidation for the hypothesis that we present regarding a transition period in late capitalism, where certain essentially modern forms of capital reproduction seem still far from disappearing. Which is not to say that in qualitative terms such forms continue to be the preponderant aspect of capitalist accumulation. In this regard, it is also a matter of a certain restriction that we point out regarding the concept of cognitive capitalism, because in the view of some of its main theorists, such as Negri, the transition to a new form of society seems already completed and without contradictions.

It is also possible to state that the idea of human capital as a form of self-exploitation refers to processes of formation, investment and mobilization of resources that are above all symbolic and, therefore, cultural. Self-qualification, whether of the wage worker or the entrepreneur, concerns the absorption of knowledge that does not always correspond directly to the possession of properties and even money. Although the latter appears in general as an end, in late capitalism economic power is not necessarily equated with symbolic and cultural power, to remember both Max Weber and Pierre Bourdieu.

To recall the latter's thesis regarding symbolic power, we see that Bourdieu refers to a certain type of capital that is not necessarily economic, but to a cultural capital that allows for a glimpse of forms of social distinction that are assimilated to the aesthetic taste of different social strata. Certain groups are recognized as belonging to a social class insofar as they carry a set of cultural qualifications that are specific to their strata, such as a taste for music, films, images, housing, and food. It seems to us that in diverse aspects the concept of human capital finds correspondence in Bourdieu's explanations about symbolic goods. His empirical studies on "taste,"[199] however, were carried out in a historical context prior to the effective manifestation of the culture of late capitalism, which in our understanding is only fully visible from the 1970s onwards.[200]

The forms of social distinction in progress today must be explained based not only on the evaluative transformation of certain signs, but on the very change that takes place in the sphere of cultural goods. What would be more important today from a symbolic point of view: lecturing about a Bertolucci film or putting your home video to be watched by millions of people on the *web*? But, even with this profound historical transformation, we are referring to the way in which certain social hierarchies are established on the margins of property ownership, leading us, to a certain extent, to Rifkin's concept of cultural capital. That is, the possibility of having access, of making use of the instrumentalization of knowledge, becomes not only a form of social distinction, but also a prerequisite for the possibility of consumption and even citizenship. The growing number of *Lan Houses,* even in the most peripheral neighborhoods of large cities in Africa or Latin America, is associated with the fact that the internet is not only an instrument for finding an employment, but also for having access to certain services, including public ones (schools, contests, documents, scheduling of health services) which, in many cases, no longer provide any other form of access, other than the network.

Perceiving the sphere of culture as the one in which the domination of late capitalism finds its most solid foundation does not mean defending a primacy of culture (of a culturalism). It means the conviction that domination continues to occur from the economic sphere, although this sphere is no longer distinguished from the cultural sphere. Immaterial labor equated its differentiations. Aspe and Combes in their concept of total mobilization,[201] critically refer to the tradition of those who continue to use concepts such as "alienation" (in this case, the Frankfurtian tradition) to explain something that would already be much more accentuated in the age of self-exploitation.

---

[199] Pierre Bourdieu, *A Distinção* (Porto Alegre: Zouk, 2007).

[200] Bourdieu's research presented in *A Distinção* were carried out in the 1960s. Although some authors such as Anderson (1999) place the origins of the so-called postmodern culture in a historical period even before the 1960s, our analysis of the cultural transformations of contemporary society is specifically refers to what began in the 1970s. See: Perry Anderson, *As Origens da Pós-Modernidade* (Rio de Janeiro: Zahar, 1999).

[201] Aspe and Combes, "Revenu."

It seems evident to us that the "subjective adhesion" that characterizes immaterial labor effectively needs new conceptual parameters for the understanding of late capitalism, but it does not seem to us that the dialectic of the particular and the universal has been overcome, at the price of saying that the Marx himself was idealist, insofar as the universality befitting the concept of capitalism continues to have its objective foundation in the *commodity itself.*

CHAPTER 8

EXPERIENCE AND CRITIQUE
IN LATE CAPITALISM

In the origin of the critical theory of society, in the 1930s, the search for a normative content, for an emancipatory interest, which was lost as a political proposition in the 1940s, was present as an inseparable component of its own concept. Later, Habermas became the center of attention in the sense of recovering that original idea that was no longer the explicit motive of Adorno and Horkheimer's thinking. Just as the idea of domination will assume a peculiar character in the versions of Habermas and Honneth, who point to the notion of pathologies of modernity, the idea of emancipation also acquires a new formulation. Our purpose in this last essay of the book is to point to the following hypothesis: just as the concept of capitalism that these authors deal with is insufficient for the understanding of a capitalism based on the prominence of immaterial labor, so too the normative content that inspires recent versions of the critical theory can find a new focus of reflection, already opened by Honneth himself, when dealing with the concept of *experience*.

From the previous statements about what we understand by late capitalism today, our objective will not be to make an exposition on how the idea of emancipation has been treated in this context, which would involve authoring another book, but rather to explore something that is suggested by at least two authors discussed so far: André Gorz and Axel Honneth. In both, and in Adorno, which we will talk about later, the concept of experience is suggested as something significant for the understanding that domination finds a limit when confronted with the force of this concept. We understand that both make this suggestion without sufficiently exploring their wealth, and their problematization finds a strong correspondence in our thesis regarding a capitalism in which culture and economy have become indistinguishable.

The central idea regarding the possibility of emancipation and even of a utopian thought under the regime of the immaterial, as we have already suggested, is manifested in the voice of the defenders of cognitive capitalism (Gorz and the thinkers of *Multitudes*), on the assumption that collective intelligence can exhibit a contradictory existence. On the one hand, capital wants to appropriate the knowledge produced by society, extending its domination to the very dimension of life, as a biopower, but at the same time the *savoir* that results from the cooperation of brains and social productivity is also an expression of the crisis current of capitalism. Capital faces the difficulty of privately appropriating this knowledge/*savoirs*, which ends up constituting a type of *knowledge communism*, which would be the basis for thinking about a new society no longer governed by the domination of capital. This formulation finds differences among cognitive theorists themselves, as we have seen in the case of Moulier-Boutang.

If we take this general idea as an expression of the emancipatory vision of those who theorize the immaterial,[202] we realize that for its authors the fate of capitalism is not simply given over to the development of productive forces, but its reality continues to be conflicting. After all, the signs of resistance are many; firstly, the collective intelligence itself, whose most mentioned expression when necessary to point out a subject is the figure of the *hacker*, but also the disputes proposed by post-socialist movements that, by detaching themselves from the forms of struggle that characterized an earlier phase of capitalism, propose changes that may constitute clear limits to the expansion of capital.

Such propositions are quite explicit in different recent books by André Gorz, including with regard to the slogans that must be raised by trade unionism itself and by the specific sphere of struggles that involve the world of labor. It is precisely in such works by Gorz that we find not only well-defined political propositions, but also the suggestion that the concept of experience plays a fundamental role in the constitution of mechanisms of resistance to capital and its economic rationality.[203] However, this suggestion does not reappear clearly in the main work of this author that we are analyzing that is *O Imaterial*. In this work Gorz no longer emphasizes the central theses explained in his two previous works, notably the two-dimensionality of rationality and society, where we find a clear relationship between emancipation and experience.

We exposed at the beginning of this work the general outlines as for Gorz's thinking about the different types of rationality that he understands

---

[202] Although we can consider that the idea of emancipation has several aspects, often antinomic, as shown by Laclau. See: Ernesto Laclau, "Beyond Emancipation," in *Emancipations, Modern and Postmodern*, Ed Jan Nederveen Pieterse, (London: Sage Publications, 1992), 121-38.

[203] See, for example: André Gorz, *Misérias do Presente, Riqueza do Possível* (São Paulo: Annablume, 2004a), and *Metamorfoses do Trabalho*.

to be present in society, which allows us to compare his thinking with that of Habermas; the relationship between autonomy and heteronomy; and the importance of the notion of time and temporality as not only a sociological but also a philosophical category. Gorz's first major political proposition, that of fighting for a reduction in labor time, does not only have the meaning of a struggle for the reduction of exploitation at labor, but has the meaning that human lifetime destined to occupy and enabling experiences that are disconnected from economic rationality is the expression of a possible autonomy. There are experiences that take place in the lifeworld that are potentially emancipatory when the actions taken by individuals show themselves as a form of resistance by them regarding their own social identity. Thus, while for Habermas in the lifeworld, individuals express an identity based on behavior consistent with certain institutionalized moral norms – insofar as they act on the basis of cultural standards that allow them to reach understanding – for Gorz, on the other hand, this lifeworld only makes possible the constitution of an autonomous subject because there are experiences that separate him from his own collective identity. According to Gorz, when arguing with Habermas about the concept of *Lebenswelt:*

> Therefore, I preferred to start from lived experience in order to explain, through existential (phenomenological) analysis, what in the original meaning (that is, in the intention) of a certain number of activities makes them incompatible with economic rationality. This difference in method makes economic rationality seem inapplicable, *from the subject's point of view* – that is, evidence based on lived understanding –, to a series of activities and relationships that cannot be subsumed under the concept of "symbolic reproduction" of the lifeworld or "communicational reason."[204]

Both in his book *Metamorfoses do Trabalho,* as in *Miséria do Presente, Riqueza do Possível,* Gorz insists that the possibility of autonomy lies in the individual expressing a certain singularity, not identifying with the norms and the group. The individual is more autonomous the more he resists, rebels, engages with creative acts and does not allow his identity to be subsumed by institutionalized norms:

> The non-coincidence of the individual-subject with the "identity" that society obliges him to (or that society provides him with the means to express) is the origin of individual autonomy and of all cultural creation. It is this that is thematized in the questioning or refusal of accepted norms and values – by the contestation of language, by the subversion of common places, by the updating of a meaning beyond all discourse and the non-sense

---

[204] Gorz, *Metamorfoses do Trabalho*, 170.

that all discourse carries with it, in short, by the artistic or intellectual creation.[205]

In his work published a few years later,[206] in a long excursus on the differences between Habermas and Touraine, he postulates again, albeit a little differently, the idea that a free subject is constituted from his moments of "not identity." His notion of experience continues to rely heavily on a dual vision of society, in which the not identical only appears in that sphere of a lifeworld, that is, as does all his thinking since *Adeus ao Proletariado* the emancipatory perspective does not have its possibility in the sphere of labor, but the emancipation *of labor itself.*

In *O Imaterial* the phenomenological formulations that mark the author's entire work no longer appear so clearly. Gorz takes up a central theme of his two previous works: the normative proposition regarding an existence income, something, incidentally, shared by most cognitive theorists. As far as social emancipation is concerned, he insists on the proposal of a basic universal income, unlinked from work with an economic purpose, which is presented as essential for the constitution of a new society. On the other hand, the path that seems fruitful, and at the same time problematic, refers to what kind of existential or cultural experience will come to predominate in a society that is moving towards what Gorz calls the communism of *savoir*.

In a society in which an increasing number of individuals need to be connected to "be in the world" or to see themselves integrated into society it is worth asking ourselves about the way in which such individuals exercise their "refusal." We certainly no longer speak of the cultural experience of modernity, as we show in our hypothesis of a post-culture industry, but of an experience that can only go through new forms of networked sociability. It is in this sense that we once again postulate the distinction between culture and knowledge/*savoir*.

Gorz's assumption is that every day *savoir*, acquired as a life experience, is communicable and potentially cooperative, resistant to the purposes of capitalist rationality, even because it cannot be quantified by measuring labor time. This *savoir* presents itself as something always positive, resulting from a creative and autonomous thought, which by its very existence is already a symptom of what will be constituted as mass intellectuality. The problem is, as we understand it, that the distinction between knowledge and *savoir* is still insufficient for us to assume the modern idea of autonomy (or

---

[205] Gorz, *Metamorfoses*, 173.
[206] Gorz, *Misérias do Presente, Riqueza do Possível.* This book was originally published in 1997.

Aufklärung), since it is also necessary to distinguish the different types of *savoirs* that are mobilized by individuals, insofar as they that since they are mainly related to what happens in the cultural sphere, we refer to a subjectivity that has been permeated by new forms of reification.

We can think, for example, that so-called *hypertext* discards the modern experience of reading, replacing it with a non-linearity, a false freedom of the reader, insofar as it ultimately deals with a system of codes already pre-programmed that only make the possibility of creative and reflective thinking even more difficult. In the same way, the activities called creative, imaginative and that make up immaterial labor, when they materialize in the production of a commodity (whether in planning, design, advertising, image) will be referring to a knowledge or *savoir* whose ultimate finality is economic production, even that no longer refers to abstract labor.

What Benjamin called the loss of experience (*Erfahrung*), when referring to modern narrative,[207] puts us in front of the kind of experience of language that accompanies immaterial labor. The emphasis given by the thinkers of *Multitudes* to the communicational aspects of society also need to be problematized in the sense that the network society tends to manifest a modification and simplification of language not visible in previous stages of the history of capitalism. When we refer to some aspects of modification in the concept of culture industry, our emphasis on the dimension of the image as a guiding model for a new aesthetic apprehension does not imply totally distinguishing it from the social process that accompanies it in the dimension of language.

While thinkers like Antonio Negri see the potential of communism in the communicational dimension, we must object that language is also susceptible to a new form of reification. In a very suggestive text, Newton Ramos-de-Oliveira address the problem of the impoverishment of language in the internet age, making mention, for example, of George Orwell's *1984*, in which one of the characteristics of his fictional city, the Oceania, was the development of a new language, *newspeak*, whose construction was an attempt to increasingly simplify communication processes: "the purpose of newspeak is not expression and communication, but to fulfill the objectives of Ingsoc and, above all, to prevent the exercise of other styles of thinking."[208]

The simplification of language, increasingly common among internet users, is also, like other artifacts of the post-culture industry, a regression of

---

[207] Walter Benjamin, "O Narrador", in *Obras Escolhidas. Vol. I* (São Paulo: Brasiliense, 1985c), 197-221.

[208] Newton Ramos-de-Oliveira, "Comunicação num mundo distópico: *Small talk –* conversas vazias", in *A Indústria Cultural Hoje,* editado por Fábio Akcelrud Durão; Antônio Zuin e Alexandre Fernandez Vaz. (São Paulo: Boitempo, 2008), 136.

autonomous thinking, or of what Adorno called *Bildung*. Jameson's analysis of a new textuality of postmodernism, in which the narrative has become fragmentary and schizophrenic, no longer graspable in a linear temporality, a phenomenon also visible in cinema from the 1980s onwards, also shows, in another context of critique, that the cultural transformations underway also point to the need for a new look at language from a critical theory of society.

But, returning to Gorz, the optimism that marks his ideas about a communism of *savoir* must be contrasted with the last chapter of *O Imaterial,* which brings his reflections on the post-human, from which we can think that the immaterial transits between a utopia and a dystopia. The making of the cyborg, which had already been announced by Donna Haraway,[209] constitutes a visible unfolding of the thesis about human capital. Artificial intelligence, which also becomes artificial life, alters even more radically what we can call experience, since its emergence, that of the cyborg, ultimately means something that goes well beyond the idea of "second nature" proposed by Lukács and the Frankfurtians. It is, in this case, a limit situation between the human and the post-human, in which the concept of experience can represent a fundamental term.

In an already classic film from the 1980s, *Blade Runner,*[210] already immensely commented, including by Jameson, we come across a narrative where a group of replicants (cyborgs), whose existence was constituted in the laboratory, at a certain moment decide to take revenge on their creators, as they were pre-programmed, among other things, to have a fixed lifespan of just four years. Unusually, they rebel and are thus pursued by Detective Deckard (H. Ford). When placed under the suspicion of being human or replicants, they are taken to a kind of interview, in which they are interrogated about different questions, and at a given moment they must talk about their past life. When the replicants are questioned as to what their memory involves, the human limit situation arises.

Although they have feelings and practically all the other qualifications of what we can call humanity, they don't have, except for the replicant Rachael (Sean Young), a past experience of life, permeated with details that mark, for example, childhood, and that in principle characterizes every human being. The film, among other curiosities, had three different endings recorded by Ridley Scott, in addition to bringing explicit mentions of Cartesian thought. The question is about the fact that the post-human (the

---

[209] See, for example: Donna Haraway, *Simians, Cyborgs and Woman: The Reinvention of Nature* (New York: Routledge, 1991).
[210] 1982 film, directed by Ridley Scott and featuring Harrison Ford as the protagonist, is a true *cult* of the 1980s.

cyborg), by constituting an artificial life, manages to have all the predicates of humanity (in fact, more strength, intelligence, and beauty) except the lived experience, singular, that demarcates an identity of the subject that is not only collective, but of a self that recognizes itself in the lived experience itself.

The phenomenological inflection of the notion of experience pointed out by Gorz, although it seeks to indicate a limit to the sociological approach itself, finds in his thought a coherent normative consequence, insofar as his propositions of reducing labor time and a sufficient universal income are supported on the assumption that it is necessary to decouple wealth from labor time. The measures that provide an extension of free time, leisure, and non-heteronomous ways of labor, focus on the possibility that free experiences can take place in a more constant way, expressing an emancipation that is not only utopian, but feasible with the present course of capitalism. On the other hand, such experiences, which in his last work he seems to identify with the concept of *savoir*, should according to our hypothesis, be more clearly elucidated as to what kind of experience actually reveals what, for example, Adorno called the "not identical". Thus, we are faced with something that we understand to be a limitation of the two-dimensional conceptions of society, both by Gorz and Habermas.

Even so, Sartre's influence on Gorz's thought surprisingly approximates him to some extent to the way in which Benjamin, and especially Adorno, treated this concept. Although the concept of experience appears in a fragmented way in the work of these authors, it plays a fundamental role in the way in which the original interest of Critical Theory, emancipation, remains alive in their works, despite all the pessimistic tones that mainly the work of Adorno came to take. In *Misérias do Presente, Riqueza do Possível*, when he begins to compare Habermas and Touraine, Gorz shows not only his admiration for the latter's ideas, but he approaches Adorno's thought when referring to the theoretical relevance of critical theory in Honneth's formulation:

> In turn, the way in which Axel Honneth reinterprets Habermas' theory innovates and renews critical theory in a fruitful way. Honneth attaches crucial importance to what Adorno called the "not identical" (...): that is, the activities and relationships by which the subject refuses to identify himself with a role, a function, or a social utility (...). For Honneth, the not identical is not simply (as for Adorno) a residual dimension; on the contrary, in modern or postmodern societies, it is a dimension of individual experience that can become central and lay the foundations, at the same time, of a critique of society and an opposition to instrumental rationality.[211]

---

[211] Gorz, *Misérias*, 147.

Walter Benjamin distinguishes between the terms *Erfahrung* and *Erlebnis* to show what he understands to be a *loss of experience*. For Benjamin *Erfahrung* refers to a type of experience that he sees weakening with modern capitalism, as he shows in the opening lines of the essay *Experiência e Pobreza*.[212] He points to the fact that modern society has lost a given spontaneous narrativity that showed a synthetic form of experience, which was at the same time a collective experience. Thus, in the narratives that were passed from one generation to another, *Erfahrung* showed itself as the art of telling, something lost by modernity. How, for example, could the elders, in a broken society, deal with the youth invoking their experience?

> Not, it is clear that the experience's stock is down, and that is in a generation that between 1914 and 1918 lived through one of the most terrifying experiences in history. Perhaps this is not as strange as it seems. At the time, it was already noticeable that the fighters had returned silently from the battlefield. Poorer in communicable experiences, not richer. The war books that flooded the literary market over the next ten years did not contain experiences transmissible by word of mouth.[213]

On the other hand, *Erlebnis* is shown as the experience of the lonely individual, reflecting a lived experience restricted to his individuality. This concept seems relevant to us precisely because it introduces, in relation to the *Lebenswelt* notion, the possibility of thinking that the lived experience in general does not necessarily indicate an autonomous action. Although Benjamin's incursion into these short essay's points to the dimension of narrativity, these considerations about the loss of experience will be quite influential on Adorno's thinking.

Also, for him, the concept of experience appears mainly in the dimension of aesthetic experience, but we understand that not only in it. For Adorno, experience in the sense of *Erfahrung* is lost in those circumstances, generalized by the administered society, in which the individual becomes incapable of perceiving in the particular the dimension of the totality, subsuming himself to the logic of identity. It is evident that Adorno is clear that this concept of experience was already present in Hegel, which, as we will see later, is the starting point for Axel Honneth's thought. In Adorno's view, experience as Hegel conceives it does not refer to an isolated experience, much less to sensitive perception as it is for empiricists like Hume but refers to something that occurs in the relationship between subjects and between them and the world. Therefore, the experience is the

---

[212] Walter Benjamin, "Experiência e Pobreza", in *Obras Escolhidas. Vol. I* (São Paulo: Brasiliense, 1985c), 114-19.
[213] Benjamin, "Experiência e Pobreza," 114.

subject facing the contradictions that are posed by reality itself, and not only by thought.[214]

But totality for Adorno is a critical and at the same time historical category, therefore, it is also false because in its objectivity the capitalist mode of production is evidenced. The true is thus the "not identical," which can be expressed in experiences that are the non-acceptance of this whole (as are for Gorz the phenomenological experiences of love, friendship, artistic creation) while refusing, even if almost unconsciously, of the totality of capitalism. What happens in late capitalism is that subjectivity becomes unable to overcome the ephemeral moment of the singular, that is, to critically relate it to the universal that manifests, for him like Marx, in the commodity form. In one of his essays on music, Adorno says:

> To summarize the difference: in Beethoven and in good serious music in general – we are not referring here to bad serious music, which can be as rigid and mechanical as popular music – the detail virtually contains the whole and leads to the exposure of the whole, at the same time that it is produced from the conception of the whole. In popular music, the relationship is fortuitous. The detail has no bearing on the whole, which appears as an extrinsic structure. [215]

What Adorno thought could still be found in the experience with the high culture of modernism could also be found in other everyday experiences, as we can learn mainly in some passages of *Mínima Moralia*, or even in his texts on music and aesthetics.[216] In an original interpretation of Adorno's thought, Honneth reconsiders the theses developed on that in *The Critique of Power* and draw a sketch of Adorno's theory of society considering the reading, mainly, of those texts not explicitly dedicated to the sociological issues. For Honneth, the Adorno concept of *social physiognomy*, present in several of his texts, makes it possible to understand Adorno's original purpose as a hermeneutic of sociocultural catastrophe, strongly inspired by the Weberian theory of the "ideal type." What Adorno proposed as a critique since his inaugural speech,[217] and which reappears in the *Negative Dialectic* as conceptual constellations, would concern the procedure adopted by him in the sense of creating a model, highlighting

---

[214] See: Theodor W. Adorno, *Tres Estudios sobre Hegel* (Madrid: Taurus, 1981).

[215] Theodor W. Adorno, "Sobre a música popular," in *Textos de Sociología*, editado por Gabriel Cohn (São Paulo: Ática, 1986b.), 119.

[216] See, specially, Theodor W. Adorno, *Minima Moralia*, (São Paulo: Ática, 1992).

[217] Theodor W. Adorno, "The Actuality of Philosophy," Telos, no 31 (Spring 1977): 120-33.

relevant aspects of bourgeois cultural barbarism, with which it was possible to create a physiognomy of what Adorno called a damaged form of life.

In examining this life damaged by exacerbated reification, Adorno was inspired by Freudian thinking, including the very concept of neurosis, to demarcate those aspects of human life that indicate suffering, while a dammed search for happiness, at the same time points to ways of not acceptance, revolt, refusal, not identity, with which individuals express them almost unconsciously in the face of the damage engendered by the catastrophe. Something remembered by Honneth about Adorno, but which also concerns Benjamin, is the constant mention he makes of childhood, even suggesting the possibility that in him there would be a "physiognomy of the capitalist way of life is anchored in a normative picture of childhood."[218] We know that Honneth, however, will develop his own model of not identity, constituting a social philosophy informed by epistemological bases different from that of the first generation of Frankfurtians.

In his most expressive book *Luta por Reconhecimento* Honneth develops his critical theory of recognition. With it, we would be taking a significant step towards the constitution of a social theory with normative content and capable of explaining, within the scope of a social philosophy, the causes, and origins of the forms of disrespect (*feelings of social disrespect*) and experiences of injustice existing in modern society, and, consequently, the origin of the resulting social conflicts. Unlike Habermas, for Honneth, emancipatory actions, as he conceives them, find a very abstract explanation. Communicative action is that aimed at obtaining understanding, through language, and in Honneth's view it would show, both empirically and in the dimension of a pre-theoretical reflection, a certain deficiency for not extending the scope of the theory to the field of its own *experience*:

> A way out of this dilemma can only be postulated by the idea of developing the communication paradigm constructed by Habermas more in the direction of his theory of intersubjectivity, in fact, as a sociological presupposition. What we mean by this, for the time being, is just the not simple proposal of equating the normative potential of social interaction with the linguistic conditions for reaching understanding free from domination. We have already pointed in this direction with the thesis that moral experiences are not originated by the restriction of linguistic

---

[218] Axel Honneth, *Pathologies of Reason: on the Legacy of Critical Theory* (New York: Columbia University Press, 2009), 70.

competences, rather, they are generated by the violation of identity claims acquired in socialization.[219]

For Honneth, what he calls moral experience replaces the analysis centered on the separation between system and lifeworld. Intersubjectivity, which continues to be the epistemological assumption of interaction, refers to a conflictual model, in which individuals act pragmatically in the universe of a struggle whose aim is not to obtain consensus, but recognition. Its intention is to formulate a theory of moral normativity capable of explaining the causes of social conflicts.

In *Luta por Reconhecimento* his key references are the young Hegel and Mead, both necessary contributions to a theory of intersubjectivity. As for Hegel, Honneth points to the fact that in his early writings on *Jena,* the German philosopher develops the thesis of a "struggle for recognition" as the starting point for the formation of the spirit, with the subjective spirit being the initial moment of constitution of the individual:

> In the first part of his philosophical analysis, Hegel's methodological procedure consists in reconstructing the process of formation of the subjective spirit, expanding it step by step so that it encompasses the necessary conditions for the self-experience of individual consciousness. The result of this reconstructive procedure must clarify what experiences, full of demands, a subject must have had in the whole before being able to conceive of himself as a person endowed with "rights" and, to that extent, be able to participate in the process institutionally regulated life of a society, that is, in the "effective spirit."[220]

To the three Hegelian moments of formation of the subjective spirit in its passage to the effective spirit, correspond three forms of recognition, guided by love, right and solidarity. To formulate and understand social injustices, and to propose a just society, it is first necessary to explain the circumstances in which situations of humiliation and injustice occur. Such situations refer to a type of experience no longer situated by the parameters of the subject's philosophy and cannot be seen as cognitive.[221] It is the experiences of non-recognition, posed by the form of intersubjectivity, that impose the struggle for recognition, as Hegel had already shown, and the legal positivity of such recognition will depend on the apprehension on the part of individuals regarding the circumstances of non-recognition:

---

[219] Axel Honneth, "The Social Dynamics of Disrespect: On the Location of Critical Theory Today." *Constellations,* Vol. 1, no 2 (1994): 262.

[220] Honneth, *Luta por Reconhecimento,* 73.

[221] Honneth, *Reification,* 40.

Honneth starts from these two main sources to build a typology formed by *three distinct forms of recognition*. Thus, for him, in the dimension of primary relationships, the form of recognition is associated with *love and friendship*; in the dimension of legal relationships, it is identified as *rights*; and in the community of value, the form of recognition is *solidarity*. For each of these dimensions, there is also a *practical relationship between the individual and the self*, which are defined respectively as *self-confidence, self-respect,* and *self-esteem*.[222]

Seeking to detach himself from Hegel's idealistic traits, Honneth finds in Mead the elements of a concept of intersubjectivity that goes beyond modern metaphysics and constitutes a kind of social psychology with empirical bases. We also perceive in his theory a conflictual model, in which the author appropriates the Foucauldian theory of action in which conflict appears as the safeguard of a subjectivity still capable of autonomy, a model that is already outlined in *The Critique of Power*. As for this influence of Foucault's theory of action, we perceive a small similarity between this aspect of his thought and the theorists of *Multitudes,* insofar as the conceptions of constituent power, multitude, molecular-global, etc., even when conceiving the passage from the disciplinary society to the control society, they continue to see the emancipatory potential of postmodernity from the Foucauldian model of action.

Honneth refuses a contextual starting point for his premises, one of the themes of his controversy with Nancy Fraser.[223] He understands that the struggle for recognition meets the multiplicity of social struggles existing in contemporary society, especially over the last three decades, what with racial injustices, gender, ethnic minorities, etc., but likewise the economic struggles, which would also have, in the search for recognition, their moral foundation.

For Honneth, a critical theory of recognition, as the new central object of Critical Theory, presupposes that all social conflict, therefore, new social movements, are based on a type of injustice that always implies a struggle for recognition. The problem is, according to our understanding, regarding the assumption that all injustice is only fully constituted in terms of its concept when there is the subjective or intersubjective perception of its agents, even if at the level of intuitive and pre-theoretical perceptions. There would thus not be a clear distinction between domination and injustice, or

---

[222] Josué Pereira da Silva, "Cidadania e Reconhecimento", in *Teoria Social e Modernidade no Brasil*, ed. Leonardo Avritzer & José Maurício Domingues (Belo Horizonte: Ed. UFMG, 2000), 125.

[223] Nancy Fraser and Axel Honneth, *Redistribution or Recognition? A Political – Philosophical Exchange* (London: Verso, 2003).

the latter would replace the former. Likewise, exploitation leads to a form of non-recognition relative to the economic sphere. But what about self-exploitation, as a conscious decision of agents who constitute themselves as human capital, would it also be a form of injustice and disrespect?

The critique made by Honneth in his first work[224] regarding a sociological deficit in Adorno's thinking, with regard to the inadequacies of his economic analysis of capitalism, reaches Honneth's own thinking. By presenting a superficial approach to the category of labor,[225] it makes little explicit the way in which instrumental rationality penetrates the current structures of capitalism. The relationship between culture and capitalist economy, so important to Frankfurtians, is also not very clearly explained when we approach culture in the sense of the production of cultural goods. Although a considerable part of his critique takes the relationship between economy and culture as a key issue, his treatment of this concept, in this case too, is much closer to Habermas. Although, according to him, recognition is something that philosophically pre-exists the distinctions between the "material" and the "symbolic," in his long debate with Fraser, culture demarcates the field of symbolic reproduction, especially with regard to explain the so-called identity policies that make up a good part of the theories about the new social movements.

Honneth and Fraser's proposition in postulating the concept of recognition (and/or redistribution) as the one around which an update of Critical Theory must necessarily pass, effectively corresponds to an order of problems that must be at the center of a normative social theory, as the new social movements are also part of the context of late capitalism. On the other hand, when he refuses the Habermasian dichotomy of system and lifeworld, Honneth approaches of Horkheimer and Adorno insofar as he recovers the concept of experience, revealing another aspect of updating Critical Theory. But, at the same time, he makes almost no reference to those experiences of suffering that have not yet manifested themselves in their historical effectiveness in terms of the constitution of collective subjects, although he addresses the way in which the notion of suffering reveals the dimension of domination and his refusal in Adorno. Even recognizing that there are those injustices that have not yet been brought to public space in his subsequent argument Honneth fails to approach types of social experience that are not necessarily struggles for recognition.

---

[224] Honneth, *The Critique.*

[225] Although, doing justice to the author, he is quite clear in admitting the need for a theory effort to understand something that was neglected by Habermas and that is fundamental for a Critical Theory. According to: Honneth, "The Social Dynamics", 267.

Above, we outlined three different views on the concept of experience, which we can call phenomenological (Gorz), dialectical (Adorno) and intersubjective (Honneth), but which to a considerable extent converge to what we can call the "original idea of Critical Theory." These are views that point to the idea highlighted by Horkheimer that emancipation depends on the apprehension of experiences situated at a pre-scientific level, where the critical theorist can perceive the social forces that characterize a given historical moment.[226] Like Horkheimer, the other three thinkers mentioned above somehow find a limitation on the part of sociology, by itself, in understanding the effective dimension of such experiences.

While Gorz and Honneth highlight the search for a clearly explained normative content from experience, Adorno allows us to think that in the sphere of culture we find the residues of a utopian thought. What we called "post-culture industry" in previous chapters does not point to the exhaustion of this thought, but on the contrary, to the need to make it explicit through contemporary forms of cultural production. However, one of the central differences between Adorno and these is placed by the centrality that occupies in all his thought the concept of totality, which was recovered in the Jamesonian interpretation of postmodernity.[227] Here the phenomenon of culture is no longer clearly distinguished from the economic one, although in Adorno the distinction continues to exist as an experience of the not identical, which points much more in the direction of what is already placed by reality, than the political-normative path to be followed adopted.

Late capitalism in a transition phase, informed by the centrality of immaterial labor, can no longer approach consumer culture and the subjectivity that permeates everyday life as "non-productive," as Gorz leads us to believe in some passages, and even Adorno in your analysis of free time. The cultural sphere, by identifying itself with the economic one, does not eliminate the contradictions that are inherent to capitalism in terms of its very concept. The type of experience in progress, envisioned by Gorz, Negri and the theorists of *Multitudes* as the constitution of a collective intelligence resistant to the powers of capital is a possibility, but which also finds its limitation. The culture that once had a greater space of autonomy, according to Adorno's criticism, by becoming directly productive, poses even greater obstacles to the recovery of the modern idea of emancipation.

If experience bears a relationship with utopia, and Jameson often suggests that it is within the scope of postmodern culture itself, its possibility also depends on the awareness of its loss. Certainly not in the

---

[226] Max Horkheimer, "Teoria Tradicional e Teoria Crítica", in *Coleção Os Pensadores* (São Paulo: Abril Cultural, 1983), 117-54.
[227] Jameson, *Pós-Modernismo*, 396.

sense pointed out by Benjamin, but in terms of something even simpler, such as the effective possibilities of imagination, creation, and reflection. These cannot be attributed without further to everything that involves immaterial labor, on the contrary, we should have the ability to distinguish between experience and reification. Although Theodor Adorno from the beginning of his thought was directly opposed to Heidegger's thought, for example, and for the rest of all phenomenology, we already have innumerable indications to affirm that the "not identical" expresses itself as a type of experience that where the ontology of the false state seems to require an authentic existence.

CONCLUSION

Capitalism has changed, but it remains capitalism. And as Sartre said in a classic text: as long as capitalism exists, Marx's thinking will remain essential. Our purpose in this little book was not to propose yet another "true" interpretation of Marx's thought, but just once again to affirm that it is difficult to understand the very concept of capitalism without resorting to it. On the other hand, we do not understand that Marxian thought is the only possible way to look at the proposed object of investigation: the economic and cultural transformations of contemporary society in the last three decades.

The critical theory of society has resisted, for more than seventy years, the most varied expressions of positivism and, mainly the insistence of the systemic logic in relegating theory to a second level in the production of knowledge, privileging, especially in Latin America, what Adorno called administrative research. In our understanding, in addition to the validity of the hypotheses presented here, the attempt to make a theory under adverse conditions is already, in some way, an approximation to Critical Theory.

As for it, our effort was made in the sense of showing that since its original idea in the 1930s, passing through different generations, one of the problems always latent and still not fully resolved, concerns the way of understanding the labor category, something that was not in the center of attention of any of the main exponents of the so-called Frankfurt School. And the problem posed in our investigation refers precisely to the fact that even though it was not made explicit by the representatives of Critical Theory, a certain idea of labor was underlying its thinkers that today has completely changed. It has changed so completely that it is no longer possible to make a Critical Theory today without studying the issues surrounding this new configuration.

It so happens that, for critical theorists, and this is also what we insistently defend here, labor has long since lost its emancipatory character, if indeed it ever had it. Labor in the modern sense and human freedom are incompatible terms. However, we are experiencing, worldwide, over the last thirty years or so, a broad transformation in the way in which labor produces capitalist wealth. This wealth can no longer be understood as a unique result of the value form, insofar as abstract labor, labor time and even wage labor relations lost their centrality in this historical period.

This does not mean the end of the labor, nor its election as a central category in ontological terms. It just means a change in terms of its modern content to the detriment of a new one, in which knowledge/*savoir* and culture become the fundamental nucleus in the valorization of commodity. As such, this valuation is no longer guided by the labor-value, opening up a gap that theory strives to understand; with some authors understanding that *savoir* is the new fundamental aspect of wealth and value, and in our understanding cultural production.

The announced and now widely reported crisis of capitalism has a lot to do with the emergence and prominence of immaterial labor. The depletion of a wealth produced on the basis of value differentiates the current type of crisis in the capitalist mode of production, in the sense that knowledge, *savoir*, and culture are not measurable commodities within the process of valorization, and it is their survival that capital has taken away. In this sense, we agree here with some thinkers of cognitive capitalism, when they understand that the current financial dimension of capitalism is a part, a way of expression, of a new form of production that is being constituted from the prominence of immaterial labor.

It is still being constituted because we understand that in this first decade of the 21st century world capitalism is going through a transitional phase, not towards socialism or communism, but apparently towards a new form of capitalism. As such, by maintaining the entrenched forms of domination engendered by the instrumental rationality of modernity, it still deserves to be called late in the sense originally proposed by Frankfurtians. But as wealth-producing labor is increasingly shifting towards immateriality, this notion of late capitalism needs to be thought of today in the light of this new historical context, without losing its double articulation: the possibility of immanent critique and the dimension of normativity.

The latter, even more than in the previous phase of capitalism, continues to lurk on all possible sides, inside and outside Critical Theory, the hope of a future in which the domination of nature does not necessarily result in the propagation of new forms of exploitation, disrespect, injustice, and the imprisonment of subjectivity. Late capitalism in a transitional phase has deepened in a singular way what Lukács and Adorno called reification, since the type of subjectivity that has permeated the new human sociability, the networked, virtual, immaterial sociability, proves to be essentially contradictory, and until now, contradictory in the sense of Adorno's negative dialectic: on the one hand, it gives indications of being able to constitute itself in what Marx in the *Grundrisse* called *general intellect*, resisting the privates tentacles of capital, on the other hand, in a less optimistic way than as the theorists of cognitive capitalism see, we understand that the possibilities of autonomous thinking, along the lines advocated by the *Enlightenment*, are more than ever failing in the face of technological barbarism.

Although Habermas, currently passing through Honneth, and in general, most of the authors that served as the basis for our investigation, somehow converge to overcome the so-called philosophy of the subject in favor of different variables of the communication paradigm and of intersubjectivity, our argument in this book, even if fighting against all the risks of dogmatism, tried to sustain a vision of capitalism in molds for many already archaic: that of dialectics. In this sense, our analysis of the intertwining between cultural production and immaterial labor as the expression of a new stage in the history of capitalism sought to be guided by the Hegelian concepts of totality and not identity. Although we admit that nowadays involves the coexistence of different modes of production, the concept of capitalism continues to be based on the reality of *the commodity form* as its central aspect, and it is from it, and not from the world of ideas, that the logical relationship between the universal and the particular.

If we think that every historical transition resembles a paradigm shift, we are faced with the very difficulties of social theory in finding concepts, categories and patterns of analysis that illuminate a reality in the process of transformation. Faced with such difficulties, perhaps positive science, including sociology, may at times have a certain humility, or goodwill, with other forms of knowledge and *savoirs*, such as art, literature and aesthetics, seeking in these not only the configuration of a renewed form of domination, but also an approximation to reality that requires a little less rigorous definition of concepts, in favor of a language and forms of experience that can be constituted as the resistance of the human himself, he now, transformed into utopia.

BIBLIOGRAPHIC REFERENCES

Abensour, Miguel. *O Novo Espírito Utópico.* Campinas: Ed. Unicamp, 1990.

Adorno, Theodor W. "The Actuality of Philosophy." *Telos,* 31 (Spring 1977): 120-33.

——. *Tres Estudios sobre Hegel.* Madrid: Taurus, 1981.

——. *Dialéctica Negativa.* Madrid: Taurus, 1984.

——. "Capitalismo Tardio ou Sociedade Industrial?" In *Sociologia,* editado por Gabriel Cohn, 62-75. São Paulo: Ática, 1986a.

——. "Sobre a música popular". In *Sociologia,* editado por Gabriel Cohn, 115-46. São Paulo: Ática, 1986b.

——. *Minima Moralia.* São Paulo: Ática, 1992.

Adorno, Theodor W., e Max Horkheimer. *Dialética do Esclarecimento.* Rio de Janeiro: Zahar, 1985.

Alexander, Jeffrey C. "Ação Coletiva, cultura e Sociedade civil: secularização, atualização, inversão, revisão e deslocamento do modelo clássico dos movimentos sociais", *Revista Brasileira de Ciências Sociais,* 13, no 37, (junho 1998): 5-32.

Anderson, Perry. *Considerações Sobre o Marxismo Ocidental.* São Paulo: Brasiliense, 1989.

——. *As Origens da Pós-Modernidade.* Rio de Janeiro: Zahar, 1999.

Aspe, Bernard et Muriel Combes. « Revenu garanti et biopolitique, » *Multitudes,* Octobre, 2004, https://www.multitudes.net/revenu-garanti-et-biopolitiique/

Azaïs, Christian, Antonella Corsani, and Patrick Dieuaide, eds., *Vers Un Capitalisme Cognitif.* Paris: L'Harmattan, 2001.

Barbrook, Richard. "A regulamentação da liberdade: liberdade de expressão, liberdade de comércio e liberdade de dádiva na rede". In *Capitalismo Cognitivo,* ed. Cocco, Giuseppe; Alexander Patez Galvão; e Gerardo Silva, 133-50. Rio de Janeiro: DP & A, 2003.

Baudrillard, Jean. *The Mirror of Production.* St. Louis: Telos Press, 1975.

Bell, Daniel. *The Coming of Post-Industrial Society.* New York: Basic Books, 1999.

Benhabib, Seyla. *Critique, Norm, and Utopia.* New York: Columbia of University Press, 1986.

Benjamin, Walter. *Sociologia,* editado por Flávio Kothe. São Paulo: Ática, 1985a.

—. "Experiência e Pobreza", In *Obras Escolhidas. Vol. I*, 114-9. São Paulo: Brasiliense, 1985b.

—. "O Narrador", In *Obras Escolhidas. Vol. I*, 197-221. São Paulo: Brasiliense, 1985c.

Bidet, Jaques et Jacques Texier, eds., *La Crise du Travail.* Paris : Presses Universitaires de France, 1995.

Bourdieu, Pierre. *O Poder Simbólico.* Rio de Janeiro: Bertrand Brasil, 2000.

—. *A Distinção.* Porto Alegre: Zouk, 2007.

Braverman, Harry. *Trabalho e Capital Monopolista.* Rio de Janeiro: Zahar, 1981.

Camargo, Sílvio. *Modernidade e Dominação: Theodor Adorno e a Teoria Social Contemporânea.* São Paulo: Annablume/Fapesp, 2006.

—. "Capitalism and Utopia in The Social Theory of André Gorz," *New Proposals: Journal of Marxism and Interdisciplinary Inquiry*, 11, no 1 (Summer 2020): 59-65.

Castells, Manuel. *A Sociedade em Rede: A era da informação. Vol. I.* São Paulo: Paz e Terra, 2006.

Cocco, Giuseppe. *Trabalho e Cidadania.* São Paulo: Cortez, 2000.

Cocco, Giuseppe, Alexander Patez Galvão; e Gerardo Silva, ed., *Capitalismo Cognitivo.* Rio de Janeiro: DP & A, 2003.

Corsani, Antonella, Maurizio Lazzarato, et Antonio Negri, *Le Bassin du travail immatériel (BTI) dans la Métropole Parisienne.* Paris : L'Harmattan, 1996.

—. « Éléments d'une rupture : l'hypothèse du capitalisme cognitif» In *Vers un capitalisme cognitif,* ed. Azaïs, Christian, Antonella Corsani, and Patrick Dieuaide, 173-89. Paris: L'Harmattan, 2000.

Debord, Guy. *A Sociedade do Espetáculo.* Rio de Janeiro: Contraponto, 1998.

Deleuze, Gilles. *Conversações 1972-1990.* Rio de Janeiro: Ed. 34, 1992.

Deleuze, Gilles, e Félix Guattari. *O Anti-Édipo: Capitalismo e Esquizofrenia.* Rio de Janeiro: Imago, 1976.

Dubet, François. *Sociologie de L'Expérience.* Paris : Editions du Seuil, 1994.

Durão, Fábio Akcelrud, Antônio Zuin, e Alexandre Fernandez Vaz, eds., *A Indústria Cultural Hoje.* São Paulo: Boitempo, 2008.

Eagleton, Terry. *The Idea of Culture.* Oxford: Blackwell Publishing, 2000.

Fausto, Ruy. "A 'Pós-Grande Indústria' nos *Grundrisse* (e Para Além Deles)". *Lua Nova*, no 19 (novembro 1989): 47-68.

Foucault, Michel. *Naissance de la Biopolitique*. Paris: Col. Hautes Etudes: Seuil/Gallimard, 2004.

Fraser, Nancy and Axel Honneth. *Redistribution or Recognition? A Political – Philosophical Exchange*. London: Verso, 2003.

Giddens, Anthony. *A Contemporary Critique of Historical Materialism*, vol. I. Berkeley: University of California Press, 1987.

Gorz, André. *Paths to Paradise*. Boston: South and Press, 1985.

—. *Adeus ao Proletariado*. Rio de Janeiro: Forense Universitária, 1987.

—. *Metamorfoses do Trabalho*. São Paulo: Annablume, 2003.

—. *Misérias do Presente, Riqueza do Possível*. São Paulo: Annablume, 2004a.

—. "Économie de la connaissance, exploitation des savoirs », Entretien réalisé par Yann Moulier Boutang et Carlo Vercellone. *Multitudes 15,* juin 2004b. https://www.cairn.info/revue-multitudes-2004-1-page-205.htm

—. *O Imaterial*. São Paulo: Annablume, 2005.

Habermas, Jürgen. "Técnica e Ciência Enquanto Ideologia". In *Textos Escolhidos - Coleção Os Pensadores*, 313-43. São Paulo: Abril Cultural, 1983.

—. *Teoría de La Acción Comunicativa*. Tomo I. Madrid: Taurus, 1987a.

—. *Teoría de La Acción Comunicativa*. Tomo II. Madrid: Taurus, 1987b.

—. *Legitimation Crisis*. Cambridge: Polity Press, 1988.

—. *Para a Reconstrução do Materialismo Histórico*. Brasiliense: São Paulo, 1990.

—. "Modernidade - Um Projeto Inacabado". In *Um Ponto Cego no Projeto Moderno de Jürgen Habermas*, editado por Otília Arantes & Paulo Eduardo Arantes, 99-124. São Paulo: Brasilense, 1992.

—. *O Discurso Filosófico da Modernidade*. Lisboa: Dom Quixote, 1998.

Haraway, Donna. *Simians, Cyborgs and Woman: The Reinvention of Nature*, New York: Routledge, 1991.

Hardt, Michael and Antonio Negri. *Empire*. Cambridge: Harvard University Press, 2000.

—. *O Trabalho de Dionísio*. Juiz de Fora: UFJF-Pazulin, 2004.

Harvey, David. *Condição Pós-Moderna. Uma Pesquisa sobre as origens da mudança cultural*. São Paulo: Loyola, 1993.

Honneth, Axel. *The Critique of Power. Reflective Stages in a critical social Theory*. London: The MIT Press, 1991.

—. "The Social Dynamics of Disrespect: On the Location of Critical Theory Today." *Constellations*, 1, no 1 (December 1994): 255-69.

—. *Luta por Reconhecimento. A Gramática Moral dos Conflitos Sociais*. São Paulo: Ed. 34, 2003.

—. *Reification: A new look at an old idea.* New York: Oxford University Press, 2008.

—. *Pathologies of Reason: on the Legacy of Critical Theory.* New York: Columbia University Press, 2009.

Horkheimer, Max. "Teoria Tradicional e Teoria Crítica". In *Coleção Os Pensadores,* 117-54. São Paulo: Abril Cultural, 1983.

Jameson, Fredric. *O Marxismo Tardio. Adorno ou a persistência da dialética.* São Paulo: UNESP, 1996.

—. *Pós-Modernismo. A Lógica Cultural do Capitalismo Tardio.* São Paulo: Ática, 1997.

—. *A Cultura do Dinheiro.* Petrópolis: Vozes, 2001a.

—. *The Cultural Turn – Selected Writings on the Postmodern: 1983-1998.* New York: Verso, 2001b.

—. "Posmodernidad y globalización", Entrevista *Archipiélago,* no 63, 2004c. http://bibliweb.sintominio.net/pensamiento.jameson

—. *Archaeologies of the Future.* London: Verso, 2005.

Jay, Martin. *La Imaginación Dialéctica.* Madrid: Taurus, 1986.

Kumar, Krishan. *Da Sociedade Pós-Industrial à Pós-Moderna.* Rio de Janeiro: Jorge Zahar, 1997.

Laclau, Ernesto. "Beyond Emancipation." In *Emancipations, Modern and Postmodern.* Edited by Jan Nederveen Pieterse, 121-38. London: Sage Publications, 1992.

Lazzarato, Maurizio. "Immaterial Labor." In *Radical Thought in Italy,* edited by Paolo Virno and e Michael Hardt, 133-46. Minneapolis : University of Minnesota Press, 1996.

—. Du pouvoir à la biopolitique. *Multitudes,* no. 1, 2000. https://www.multitudes.net/Du-biopouvoir-a-la-biopolitique/

—. *As Revoluções do Capitalismo.* Rio de Janeiro: Civilização Brasileira, 2007.

Lazzarato, Maurizio e Antonio Negri. *Trabalho Imaterial.* Rio de Janeiro: DP & A editora, 2001.

Lévy, Pierre. *A Inteligência Coletiva.* São Paulo: Loyola, 2007.

Lukács, Georg. *História e Consciência de Classe.* Lisboa: Escorpião, 1986.

Mandel, Ernest. *O Capitalismo Tardio*: São Paulo: Abril Cultural, 1982.

Marramao, Giacomo. *O Político e as Transformações.* Belo Horizonte: Oficina de Livros, 1990.

Marcuse, Herbert. *A Ideologia da Sociedade Industrial.* Rio de Janeiro: Zahar, 1978.

—. *Eros e Civilização.* São Paulo: Círculo do Livro, 1982.

Marx, Karl. *Contribuição para a Crítica da Economia Política.* Lisboa: Estampa, 1977.

—. *Manuscritos Econômico-Filosóficos.* Lisboa: Ed.70, 1980.

—. *Crítica da Filosofia do Direito de Hegel.* Lisboa; Estampa, 1983.

—. *O Capital.* Vol. I, Livro Primeiro. São Paulo: Nova Cultural, 1985a.

—. *O Capital.* Capítulo VI (Inédito). São Paulo: Moraes, 1985b.

—. *Grundrisse: Foundations of the Critique of Political Economy.* Middlesex: Penguin Books, 1989.

—. *Wage Labour and Capital/Wages, Price and Profit.* Paris: Foreign Languages Press, 2000.

Marx, Karl, and Frederick Engels. *The German Ideology. Part One.* New York: International Publishers, 1977.

Moulier-Boutang, Yann. *Le Capitalisme Cognitif.* Paris: Éditions Amsterdam, 2007.

—. « La troisième transition du capitalisme : exode du travail productif et externalités ». In Azaïs, Christian, Antonella Corsani, and Patrick Dieuaide, eds, *Vers Un Capitalisme Cognitif,* 135-52. Paris : L'Harmattan, 2001.

Negri, Antonio. *Marx beyond Marx. Lessons on the Grundrisse.* New York: Autonomedia/Pluto, 1991.

Offe, Claus. *Capitalismo Desorganizado.* São Paulo: Brasiliense, 1995.

Pieterse, Jan Nederveen. *Emancipations, Modern and Postmodern.* London: Sage Publications, 1992.

Pollock, Frederick. "State Capitalism: Its Possibilities and Limitations." In *Critical Theory and Society – A Reader,* edited by Stephen Bronner and Douglas Kellner, 95-118. New York: Routledge, 1989.

Postone, Moishe. "Necessity, Labor, and Time: a reinterpretation of the Marxian critique of capitalism," *Social Research*, 45 (Winter 1978): 739-88.

—. *Time, Labor, and Social Domination.* London: Cambridge University Press, 2003.

Ramos de Oliveira, Newton. "Comunicação num mundo distópico: *Small talk* – conversas vazias". In *A Indústria cultural hoje,* editado por Fábio Akcelrud Durão, Antônio Zuin e Alexandre Fernandez Vaz, 125-38. São Paulo: Boitempo, 2008.

Rifkin, Jeremy. *A Era do Acesso.* São Paulo: Makron Books, 2001.

Sherman, David. "The Ontological Need: positing subjectivity and resistance in Hardt and Negri's Empire." *Telos,* 128 (Summer 2004): 143-70.

Silva, Josué Pereira da. "Cidadania e Reconhecimento". In *Teoria Social e Modernidade no Brasil,* editado por Leonardo Avritzer José Maurício Domingues, 123-35. Belo Horizonte: Ed. UFMG, 2000.

—. *Trabalho, Cidadania e Reconhecimento.* São Paulo: Annablume, 2008.

Soja, Edward W. *Geografias Pós-Modernas*. Rio de Janeiro: Zahar, 1993.

Tronti, Mário. *Operários e Capital*. Porto: Afrontamento, 1976.

Vercellone, Carlo. « Sens et enjeux de la transition vers le capitalisme cognitif : une mise en perspective historique ». *Multitudes*, Octobre, 2004. https://www.multitudes.net/Sens-et-enjeux-de-la-transition/

—. "É na reversão das relações de saber e poder que se encontra o principal fator da passagem do capitalismo industrial ao capitalismo cognitivo". Entrevista para Revista *IHU online*, no 216. São Leopoldo, abril de 2007a. https://www.ihuonline.unisinos.br/artigo/21-artigo-2007/852-carlo-vercellone-1

—. "From Formal Subsumption to General Intellect: Elements for a Marxist Reading of the Thesis of Cognitive Capitalism." *Historical Materialism*, 15, no 1, (2007b): 13-36.

Virno, Paolo. "The Ambivalence of Disenchantment," In *Radical Thought in Italy*, edited by Paolo Virno and Michael Hardt, 13-36. Minneapolis: University of Minnesota Press, 1996.

Weber, Max. *Economia e Sociedade*. Vols. I e II. São Paulo: Ed. UNB, 2004.

Williams, Raymond. *Cultura*. São Paulo: Paz e Terra, 2000.